UNDERSTANDING LANGUAGE

A Primer for the Language Arts Teacher

UNDERSTANDING LANGUAGE

A Primer for the Language Arts Teacher

Jean Malmstrom

ST. MARTIN'S PRESS
New York

In memory of my mother,
Katharine Lally Lebens,
the best language arts teacher
I have ever known

Acknowledgements

"Arithmetic" by Carl Sandburg. From COMPLETE POEMS, copyright, 1950, by Carl Sandburg. Reprinted by permission of Harcourt Brace Jovanovich, Inc.

"A Cliché" by Eve Merriam. Copyright © 1964 by Eve Merriam. From IT DOESN'T ALWAYS HAVE TO RHYME. Used by permission of Atheneum Publishers.

Library of Congress Catalog Card Number: 76–28138
Copyright © 1977 by St. Martin's Press, Inc.
Manufactured in the United States of America.

0987
fedcba

For information, write: St. Martin's Press, Inc.,
175 Fifth Avenue, New York, N.Y. 10010

Cover design: Melissa Tardiff

ISBN: cloth 0–312–83090–4
       paper 0–312–83125–0

Preface

Understanding Language: A Primer for the Language Arts Teacher aims to bridge the gap between language arts teaching and linguistic theory. Too often teachers and student teachers are expected to close this gap unaided. They may receive instruction in linguistics as well as in teaching methods, but rarely are they shown how to integrate the two—unifying the practical and the theoretical. The two parts of this book attempt to accomplish this objective.

Part One, "Information for Language Arts Teachers About Language and Linguistics" (chapters 1 through 5), presents selected aspects of linguistics that are relevant to language arts teaching. The first chapter discusses the acquisition and development of language during childhood. The second chapter explains the English sound system and how it relates to spellings and meanings. The third chapter considers grammars, presenting a composite of information selected from traditional, structural, and transformational grammars as they are relevant to language arts teaching. This grammar composite is equipment for adult teachers, not young children. Its purpose is to create grammatically self-confident language arts teachers who can introduce grammatical insights through casual gamelike activities, thus laying the foundation for their students' later comprehension of grammatical abstractions. The fourth chapter presents background information about the history of the English language, and the fifth then deals with its dialects, dictionaries, and usage.

Part Two "Applications of Linguistics to Language Arts Teaching" (chapters 6, 7, and 8), explains and demonstrates how teachers can use the linguistic information presented in Part One while teaching the three main areas of language arts. Chapter six applies linguistics to the teaching of reading; chapter seven to the teaching of literature; chapter eight, to the teaching of writing.

The appendix offers a "Language Arts Textbook Evaluation," which applies the information given in Part One and Part Two to the detailed analysis and evaluation of language arts textbooks. Although teachers are often called upon to perform this function, they usually lack specific criteria for doing so intelligently and thoroughly.

Finally, language arts teachers can consult the annotated bibliography of books and articles which supplement and reinforce the ideas contained in this book.

I thank the many language arts teachers who have helped in developing and testing the ideas presented in this book. In the preparation of the final manuscript, Susan Holaday, Jan Przbylski, and my editors at St. Martin's, Patricia Klossner and Martha Goldstein, gave essential professional assistance. I am especially grateful to them. In addition, I sincerely thank Thomas Broadbent and Judy Barrechia for their long-enduring recognition of the need for this book. Finally, mt deepest gratitude, as usual, goes to my husband, Vincent F. Malmstrom, who believed unfalteringly in the book and gently persuaded me to write it.

Jean Malmstrom

Contents

PART ONE

INFORMATION FOR LANGUAGE ARTS TEACHERS ABOUT LANGUAGE AND LINGUISTICS

1

Language Acquisition and Development

OVERVIEW AND PURPOSE OF THE CHAPTER

Linguists are scholars who study language—its history, its universal principles, and its relationships to other aspects of life. Their field of study is broadly termed *linguistics* and their chief objective is the advancement of linguistic theory. In other words, they consider themselves "pure" scientists, and they are usually not concerned about the application of their theories to the teaching of language arts—or to any other practical applications. Linguistically trained curriculum developers, textbook writers, and teachers are depended upon for these, a fact explaining the need for this book.

For almost a century linguists have been investigating how children learn language. In the 1940s a new discipline developed that combined knowledge and insights from both psychology and linguistics. In those years a union was established between behavioral psychology and structural linguistics, and *psycholinguistics* emerged emphasizing observable human behavior and language patterns.

In the late 1950s another version of psycholinguistics developed from a union of cognitive psychology and transformational–generative linguistics. Cognitive psychology emphasized the mental aspects of language learning, which cannot be observed directly. Transformational–generative linguistics also emphasized the mind, especially its innate competence to learn and use language. Experts in both fields agreed that the human mind can be studied and that one of the best ways to study it is through the language system it uses. Psycholinguists then emphasized the powerful regularities of the underlying language system rather than its surface differences in actual realized sentences.

Teachers are introduced to some of the dynamic insights developed by linguists and psycholinguists in this chapter. These insights can improve the teaching of the language arts by helping with wise day-by-day answers to such basic questions as:

1.   What are my teaching priorities?
2.   How can I individualize instruction?

By the time children enter school, they can usually send and receive spoken messages in some language. In other words, their first communication skills—listening and speaking—are learned without formal instruction, merely by their having lived in a language-rich environment. When children send and receive messages in spoken language, they prove that they have internalized a working grammar of their native language. Although they do not yet possess full control of all adult grammar structures, they do command the basic structures, or rules, of their native language. Therefore, language arts teachers do not need to instruct children about language the same way that historical facts are taught by social studies teachers, or arithmetical processes are taught by math teachers. Instead, the language arts teacher can concentrate on helping children with their various problems in learning to read and write while working to enrich their experiences with literature and creative activities, both oral and written.

Furthermore, linguists tell us that, for example, all English-speaking children learn the same basic language patterns and structures. Nevertheless, in the actual articulated sentences that children speak, there may be variations in pronunciation or in their choices of words and phrases. Such surface structure differences are associated with dialects. Linguists define *dialects* as varieties of language reflecting the speakers' regional and social backgrounds. Linguistically informed teachers respect children's dialects because they know that children speak as they have heard the language spoken. As adults, we speak many dialects, skillfully varying them according to the situation in which we find ourselves. As teachers, we want children to learn this sensitivity to appropriate ways of speaking and writing.

The truly important fact about dialects is that their similarities far outnumber and outweigh their differences. Linguistically informed teachers play down differences and emphasize similarities. They use whatever dialect the child brings to the classroom as a starting point for teaching communication. Recognizing each child's relatively few problem areas, the teacher works individually on these areas.

Psycholinguistic insights persuade teachers to respect the amazing grammatical competence of children. Without such respect, children may be irreparably injured in their school experience. Therefore, this chapter examines the stages through which children achieve their grammatical competence: (1) early cognitive development, (2) early language development, and (3) building a grammar by developing basic sentence patterns and transformations.

EARLY COGNITIVE DEVELOPMENT

In studying infants' behavior before they learn to speak, psychologists have seriously considered the question: which comes first, *thought* or *language*? Modern psycholinguistics generally hold that language is an example of children's mental development, of their ability to think. Language is an innate part of human nature.

The ability to learn and use language distinguishes human beings from all other living beings. Language is a system of symbols used by human beings to communicate a limitless range of meanings to other human beings who use the same symbol system. Children's prespeech behavior reveals their inherent ability to symbolize. For example, when children pretend that a blanket draped over a chair is a house, they demonstrate their "knowledge" about houses and about how to use a chair and a blanket to symbolize key features of houses, as they perceive them in their environment. Such play reveals the human ability of children to symbolize concrete and abstract meanings.

In developing their power to symbolize, infants first categorize information perceived from their environment by means of their five senses—seeing, hearing, smelling, tasting, and touching. For example, by all these senses infants learn to distinguish people from toys. Within the people category, they soon learn to separate Mommy from Brother, ignoring their shared humanness but recognizing their mutual differences. Thus they gradually subcategorize information and organize their world more accurately.

Next infants begin to discover that people around them use similar categories and subcategories. They notice, for example, that other people also have shoes—which are things people wear on their feet—even though they may be called *sneakers, boots, slippers,* or *sandals,* as well as *shoes.*

Once children learn that objects have distinctive names, they acquire the power to use names without being distracted by irrelevant secondary features. For example, they learn that the word *shoe* refers equally well to their white canvas sneakers, Mommy's red leather slippers, and Daddy's black rubber boots. The secondary features—*white, canvas, red, leather, black,* and *rubber*—specify the subcategories of the major cognitive category *shoe.* Children learn that the category *shoe* covers these subcategories.

In addition to learning that objects with shared features have the same name—*shoe, car, toy*—they also learn that objects with unique features have unique names—*Susan, Fred, Fluffy, Bozo.* The cognitive structure that children use for categorizing their environment adds meaning to their language.

EARLY LANGUAGE DEVELOPMENT

Normal children pass through the same stages of language learning, although at widely differing rates of speed. When infants are about twelve months old they usually learn to use one-word utterances which are often called *holophrastic speech*. These word utterances name people, animals, objects, and events in the child's environment—*baby, kitty, milk, all-gone*; or they are exclamations like *Byebye, Hi, No*; or they are commands like *Up! Down!* or *Come!*

At this stage children can use normal sentence intonations on their single-word utterances. For example, the word *Daddy* can be used to mean "Here's Daddy." "Is Daddy here?" or "Come here, Daddy!" The music and rhythm the children use in saying the word communicates its intended meaning to the listener. In the holophrastic stage, then, there is a one-to-one correlation between the word and its real-world referent. That is, the word *Daddy* is simultaneously a one-word sentence and a person.

In the next stage of early language development—beginning around eighteen months—children discover that adding extra words creates clearer meaning. They experiment with putting words together and use syntax, or grammar, in its simplest form. During this stage they are making a transition from a one-to-one correlation between word and its referent to a much more complicated word-to-word connection within language itself. For example, if we listen to the monologues of a two-year-old child playing alone or just before falling asleep, we hear much self-directed practice in putting words together, like a student drilling in a language laboratory.

Here are some substitution drills from presleep monologues of two-and-a-half year old Anthony.

> "What color—What color blanket—What color mop—
> What color glass . . . Not the yellow blanket—The
> white . . .
> It's not black—It's yellow . . . Not yellow—Red . . .
> Put on a blanket—Yellow light . . . There is the light—
> Where is the light—Here is the light."[1]

A detailed study of Anthony's speech revealed that he also used "build-ups," "breakdowns," and "completions."

> Build-up: Sit down . . . Sit down on the blanket.
> Breakdown: Anthony jump down . . . Anthony jump.
> Completion: And put it . . . Up there.

At this stage there are frequent references to self and Mommy, and to three basic operations that can be performed by language:

1. Nomination—signaled by such words as *this, that, see, there*
2. Recurrence—signaled by such words as *more* and *another*
3. Nonexistence—signaled by such words as *all-gone, no.*

Uninflected verbs and descriptive adjectives are present at this stage (as we have seen above), and nouns appear in various semantic relationships with verbs. Some of these relationships are:

> agent—action (as in *Mommy fix*)
> agent—action—object (as in *I ride horsie*)
> action—object—location (as in *Put truck window*)
> agent—action—object—location (as in *Adam put it box*)[2]

Even at this early stage of development, the child is using language with the essentially human purpose of communicating meaning and not merely of naming objects. The child is asserting the existence of consistent relationships in the environment.

Moreover, when children hesitate and repeat utterances like *Adam put it box:*

> Put it . . . Adam put it . . . Adam put it . . . box

they reveal a growing understanding of the sentence structure of their language. They have separated the sentence into its parts. They know the subject—*Adam*—from the predicate—*put it box.* Furthermore, within the predicate, the hesitation between *put it* and *box* shows that they have subdivided the predicate into verb + object—*put it*—from the location—*box.*

Such speech is often called *telegraphic* because it concentrates on nouns, verbs, and descriptive adjectives, which have their own semantic content. It usually omits function words like prepositions, articles, and conjunctions. These words have little or no semantic content but merely show how the content words are related to each other.

In the next stage of language acquisition, children learn to use grammatical morphemes, the smallest significant units of syntax. These may be either words or parts of words. For example, the idea of possession may be expressed either by the preposition *of* (*the decision of the court*) or by the suffix *'s* or *s'* (*the court's decision* or *both the courts' decision*). Both *of* and *'s* (or *s'*) are grammatical morphemes expressing possession.

Apparently, grammatical morphemes are acquired in a remarkably predictable sequence by English-speaking children. The following chart summarizes the findings of leading investigators and shows that, with only minor variations, the children whom they had studied followed a consistent order in learning fourteen crucial grammatical morphemes.

1. Present progressive –*ing* (Bobo sleep*ing*)
2. and 3. *in* and *on* (*in box, on table*)
4. Plural –*s* (*toys*)
5. Past irregular (*went, broke*)
6. Possessive (Anthony*'s* blanket)
7. Uncontractible linking verb *is* (*Is* the blanket yellow?)
8. Articles *the, a, an*
9. Past Regular –*ed* (*played*)
10. Third person regular –*s* (*plays*)
11. Third person irregular –*s* (*does, has*)
12. Uncontractible auxiliary *is* (*Is* Daddy sleeping?)
13. Contractible linking verb –*s* (Daddy*'s* hungry)
14. Contractible auxiliary –*s* (Blacky*'s* barking)[3]

Although this order of learning appears consistent, the rate of learning varies greatly and may extend into the seventh or eighth year. However, many of these morphemes are clearly present in the speech of preschool children. One investigator demonstrated this truth by showing preschool children pictures of imaginary creatures, objects, and actions with nonsense names. The children could use plural, possessive, and third person regular suffixes with skill.[4]

All stages in early language development lead toward the ultimate goal: an adult grammar. Studies show that very young children learning different languages encounter the same stages in language development as do English-speaking children. The same fourteen relationships account for practically every utterance. Typical examples are nominative (*that dog*), possessive (*Mommy shoe*), locative (*go home*), and attributive (*big ball*). These consistencies reveal the nature and extent of the cognitive growth of children everywhere. Children who are just beginning to speak seem to express what they already know about their world.

DEVELOPING A GRAMMAR

Many, if not most, recent studies of children's language learning are based in transformational–grammatical theory (to be discussed in chapter 3). At this point we will consider some useful insights the theory offers for understanding children's developing knowledge of their language.

In the first three years of their life, children begin to grasp the system underlying their language. As we have seen, they build the base structure rules needed to clarify the meanings of sentences. They learn that nouns are marked by the articles *the, a,* and *an,* and that they are regularly inflected for plural by *–s.* They learn that verbs are marked for number and tense and are often preceded by auxiliaries. In the process of this learning, children often have to master subcategories like the irregular noun plurals *children, men,* and *women.* In the verb area, they often master irregular forms like *went* and *broke* before learning the rule about the regular past suffix *–ed.* Once they have learned this rule, they sometimes overextend it to irregular verbs, producing *goed* and *breaked* on the analogy of the regular pattern. In such cases, children must relearn the irregular patterns either by correction from older speakers or by hearing mature speech.

Simple Transformations

Even in the earliest stages of their language development, children learn to produce negatives and questions through simple transformations as well as by intonation patterns. In learning simple transformations, children progress through stages of accuracy toward completely grammatical forms. Here is a set showing a progression for Yes–No questions, WH questions and Negatives.

> Yes–No questions: *This powder? This is powder? Is this is the powder? Is this the powder?*
> WH questions: *Where goes the wheel? Where the wheel goes? Where the wheel do go? Where does the wheel goes? Where does the wheel go?*
> Negatives: *No touch. I not touch. I'm not touching.*[5]

Other simple transformations used by three year olds are:

1. Reflexive   *He washed himself*
2. Passive   *Blackie got spanked*
3. Adverb movement *Now I want to color, here's the book*
4. There   *There will be a lot of trouble*
5. Verb particle   *She took that rouge off, she put them on.*[6]

Complex Transformations

Children soon learn that language processes are recursive, or repetitive. They discover that simple sentences can fit together to make compound and complex sentences, and that this process can occur over and over again to create longer and longer sentences. By conjoining and inserting short sentences, children learn to make long sentences. Thus they add complex transformations to their grammar.

In this process conjoining precedes inserting, because conjoining retains the word order of the original conjoined sentences, whereas inserting often requires changes in word order as well as deletions and substitutions. First graders can produce conjoined sentences like the following.

> Wendy and he wanted them to be a mother
> My brother doesn't play with me but she hits me
> Don't take that out or you would get in trouble.[7]

Although these sentences show some slightly offbeat structures, the children do understand the process of conjoining.

Before they are seven, children learn to insert infinitive nominalizations:

> *I want to play.*

At about the same age, they learn to insert relative clauses in sentences like the following.

> The lady *who was here yesterday* came back.

Relatives standing at the end of the sentence are learned much earlier:

> I saw the lady *who was here yesterday.*

Children also master other forms of adjectivalization such as possessives—*Anthony's blanket*—and prenoun adjectives like *red car.* These are reduced adjectivalizations, which are theoretically more complex than relative clause inserts. Yet children have no trouble learning them, probably because they are frequently used in ordinary speech.

Other complex distinctions make their appearance later in children's speech development. Four of them were investigated and discovered to be absent in the comprehension of five year olds but present by age ten.[8] These are the distinctions acquired during that five-year period:

1. The difference in meaning between *John is eager to see* and *John is easy to see.*

In the first sentence John is the person doing the seeing; in the second, John is the person being seen. Yet the surface structures of the two sentences are identical except for the differing adjectives *eager* and *easy.*

2. The difference between *John promised Bill to leave* and *John told Bill to leave.*

In the first sentence John is the one who is supposed to leave; in the second, Bill is the one who is supposed to leave.

3. The difference between *John asked Bill what to do* and *John told Bill what to do.*

In the first sentence, John is the one who is going to do something; in the second, Bill is the one.

4. The correct interpretations of pronouns in sentences like:
   a. He found out that Mickey won the race.
   b. After he got the candy, Mickey left.
   c. Pluto thinks he knows everything.

In a, the pronoun *he* must refer to someone outside the sentence. In b and c, the pronoun *he* can refer either to Mickey and Pluto respectively or to someone outside the sentence. The pronoun problems were the easiest for the children to learn. By five and six months all understood the pronoun usages.

These grammatical areas are exceptional; teachers of primary grades can concentrate on these in helping children learn transformations. The job of mastering such exceptional rules seems to be a process of individual learning. By supplying ample opportunity for interesting conversations, the elementary teacher can gradually help children to grasp the remaining grammatical rules that underlie fully adult grammars.

However, no matter how much we learn about language, there is always more to know. Basic rules and transformations are the essential beginning; meanings extend infinitely. No two people have identical semantic patterns in their minds. Moreover language constantly changes just as people change. These facts lend challenge and excitement to the psycholinguistic study of language and especially to language learning.

SUGGESTIONS FOR STUDY AND DISCUSSION

1. In the light of this chapter, how might you explain the fact that ten-year-old children can often understand a younger brother or sister more easily than the parents can?

2. Why is communication between human beings different from communication between human beings and animals?

3. If possible, record the vocal sounds made by a baby in the first years of life. How well could the standard alphabet be used to "spell" these utterances? How intelligible are the child's intonation patterns?

4. Why are there no dictionaries listing English sentences in the way word dictionaries list words?

5. Many studies of child language have been based on evidence obtained during carefully structured interviews or tests. Others have been based on evidence recorded from the free speech of children in their home environment. What advantages might each method have? If possible, test your conclusions with preschool children, three to four years old.

NOTES

[1] Ruth Weir, *Language in the Crib* (The Hague: Mouton, 1962), p. 19.

[2] Roger Brown, *A First Language: The Early Stages* (Cambridge, Mass.: Harvard University Press, 1973), p. 205.

[3] Ibid., p. 281.

[4] Jean Berko Gleason, "The Child's Learning of Morphology," *Word* 14 (1958), 150–177.

[5] Adapted from Paula Menyuk's, *Sentences Children Use* (Cambridge, Mass.: M.I.T. Press, 1969), p. 73.

[6] Adapted from Paula Menyuk's, *The Acquisition and Development of Language* (Englewood Cliffs, N.J.: Prentice-Hall, 1971), p. 140.

[7] Ibid., p. 146.

[8] Carol Chomsky, *The Acquisition of Syntax in Children from 5 to 10* (Cambridge, Mass.: M.I.T. Press, 1969), pp. 24–112.

2

Relationships Among Sounds, Spellings, and Meanings

OVERVIEW AND PURPOSE OF THE CHAPTER

A linguistically based understanding of the sound system of English can be used by language arts teachers in teaching both reading and writing. Sounds and letters communicate language meaning only when they occur in the contexts of words, phrases, and sentences. Therefore, linguistically informed teachers encourage students to use context clues not only to read for meaning but also to achieve spelling power in writing.

Such teachers do not fall victim to the common fallacy that "letters have sounds." For example, they do not write the letter k on the board and ask their students, "What does that letter say?" This question is answerable only in a specific written context. Otherwise children cannot know for sure whether the teacher expects the sound of k in kick and king or the silence of k in knot or knob. The teacher may even want the name of the letter, pronounced "kay," as the personal name.

The wise language arts teacher begins by focusing the students' attention on the regularities in the English spelling system. Later, the children can concentrate on predictable irregularities and finally, upon the relatively few true irregularities. For example, the irregular word may be of foreign origin, like *chaos* from Greek or *chef* from French. Or the spelling may be a historical accident, like *island* instead of the earlier and more logical spelling *iland*, or *debt* instead of the Middle English spelling *dette*.

Recognizing these values, this chapter explains: (1) how sounds and letters differ, (2) how the human vocal organs produce sounds, (3) how speech sounds are organized into meaningful units, and (4) how to use these three linguistic insights in teaching spelling.

HOW SOUNDS AND LETTERS DIFFER

Linguistically informed teachers carefully distinguish between sounds and letters. To keep this distinction clear, this book shows *letters* (called "graphemes" by linguists) printed in italics. On the other hand, *sounds* (often called "phonemes" by linguists) are framed between slant lines. Thus the graphemes *p*, *v*, and *d* are clearly distinguished from the phonemes /p/, /v/, and /d/.

Spoken English uses about thirty-five phonemes, but the English alphabet contains only twenty-six graphemes. Consequently, one grapheme may represent more than one phoneme (as *c* represents /k/ in *case* but /s/ in *celery*). In addition, one phoneme may be represented by more than one grapheme (as /f/ is represented by *f* in *face* but *ph* in *phone*). In all, there are about two thousand ways to spell the phonemes of English. Clearly, there is no one-to-one correspondence between phonemes and graphemes. If we wish to establish correspondence, we need a phonetic or phonemic alphabet in which one written symbol consistently represents one and only one spoken sound. Two of the most widely used such alphabets are the International Phonetic Alphabet (IPA) and the Trager–Smith Phonemic Alphabet.

The difference between phonetic and phonemic alphabets centers in the fact that each language has its own set of meaningful sounds. To record every sound distinctively, the International Phonetic Alphabet was formulated in the late nineteenth century. It purposed to have a symbol to record every sound of every language in the world. If a new sound were found, a new symbol would be invented. However, later research showed that no two speech sounds are identical. Nevertheless, listeners organize these raw data of speech into significant sound units, or phonemes, of their language. The same basic principle of organization can be applied to letters in writing. We can write and print the letter p in many forms:

P, p, P, p, 𝒫, 𝓅.

Each symbol is different, but we organize them mentally into one meaningful unit of writing, the grapheme p.

The alphabet presented in Figure 2–1 is the Trager–Smith Phonemic Alphabet, invented by the structural linguists George L. Trager and Henry Lee Smith, Jr., for recording the phonemes of American English. A phonemic alphabet records only the phonemes, or significant sound classes, of one particular language. It is therefore shorter and simpler than a phonetic alphabet but quite sufficient for the purposes of this book.

HOW SOUNDS ARE PRODUCED

Human beings produce speech sounds by means of their vocal organs. Air issues from the lungs, passes through the space between the vocal cords in the throat, and passes out of the body through either the mouth or the nose. In the process, the resonators intensify it and the articulators shape the sound in various ways. The resonators are the pharynx (or pharyngeal cavity), the mouth (or oral cavity), and the nose (or nasal cavity). The articulators are the soft palate (or velum), the hard palate, the tongue, the teeth, and the lips.

Vowels:

	Front	Central	Back
High	i	ɨ	u
Mid	e	ə	o
Low	æ	a	ɔ

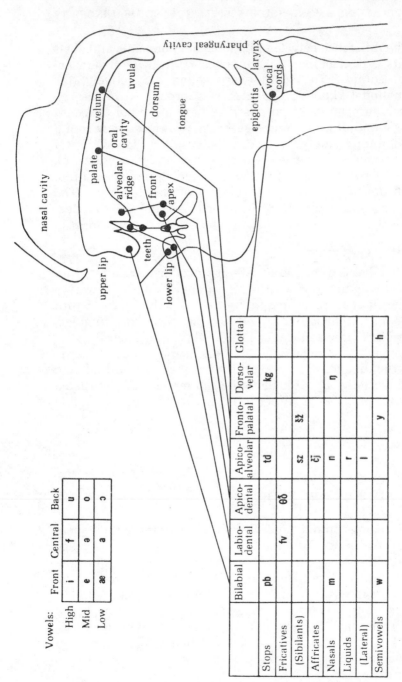

	Bilabial	Labio-dental	Apico-dental	Apico-alveolar	Fronto-palatal	Dorso-velar	Glottal
Stops	pb			td		kg	
Fricatives		fv	θð				
(Sibilants)				sz	šž		
Affricates				čj			
Nasals	m			n		ŋ	
Liquids				r			
(Lateral)				l			
Semivowels	w				y		h

FIGURE 2–1

SOURCE. Adapted from Coursebook for English Language, 1966–1967, Western Michigan University, by permission of Bernadine P. Carlson.

Figure 2–1 locates the consonant sounds according to their articulators and points of articulation, and keys the sounds to the descriptions of how they are produced. Bilabial consonants /p, b, m/, as in pet, bet, met, are produced by the two lips. Labiodental consonants /f, v/, as in fat and vat, are produced by the lower lip and the upper teeth. Apicodental consonants /θ, ð/, as in thin and then, are produced by the apex of the tongue and the upper teeth. Apicoalveolar consonants /t, d, s, z, č, ǰ, n, r, l/, as in ten, den, sip, zip, church, jump, no, run, love, are produced by the tip ("apex") of the tongue and the alveolar ridge. Frontopalatal consonants /š, ž/, as in she and pleasure, are produced by the front of the tongue and the hard palate. Dorsovelar consonants /k, g, ŋ/, as in kin, get, ring, are produced by the back ("dorsum") of the tongue and the velum.

Many English consonants occur in voiceless–voiced pairs. Voicing occurs when the breath stream is restricted by the partial closing of the glottis (the space between the vocal cords), with resulting tension and vibration of the vocal cords. The vibration is termed voice; the resulting sound is voiced. When the vocal cords are open and relaxed, the breath can pass through the glottis without causing the vocal cords to vibrate. The resulting sound is voiceless, or unvoiced. Voicing can be detected by pressing the fingers to the "Adam's Apple" or by plugging the ears with two fingers while pronouncing a voiceless–voiced pair like pin-bin or tan-Dan.

In figure 2–1, these consonant pairs are shown together. In each pair the first consonant is voiceless, the second, voiced. The column headings show the sounds' points of articulation, from the bilabial position at the front of the mouth to the glottal position in the throat. The left-hand column indicates how the breath is modified when the sound pairs are pronounced. Stops are produced by a momentary blockage of the breath. Fricatives and their subclass sibilants permit the breath to issue from the mouth through variously shaped narrow openings producing a friction or hissing noise. Affricates almost simultaneously combine the features of stops and fricatives. With all these sounds the breath issues through the mouth. In the case of the three nasals, however, the breath issues from the nose. All English nasals are voiced. With liquids, and their subclass laterals, the tongue may touch the roof of the mouth but does not stop the breath or produce a friction or hissing sound. English liquids are voiced.

English sounds divide into consonants, which are characterized by being blocked or restricted in the breath channel and vowels, which are not blocked or restricted. Vowels resonate in the oral cavity. The tongue shapes the mouth variously to produce different vowels. Such shapings are classified horizontally as *front* ("front of the mouth"), *central*, or *back* and vertically as *high* ("high in the mouth"), *mid*, or *low*, as shown by the small rectangle at the upper left of figure 2–1. The following is the Trager–Smith analysis of the nine "pure" vowel phonemes.

High front /i/	as in *b*it
Mid front /e/	as in *b*et
Low front ("ash") /æ/	as in *b*at
High central ("barred i") /ɨ/	as in the adverb *j*ust
Mid central ("schwa") /ə/	as in *a*bove
Low central /a/	as in *f*ather
High back /u/	as in *b*ook
Mid back /o/	In American English occurs only followed by /w/ or /y/
Low back /ɔ/ ("open o")	as in *b*ought

The last line of the consonant chart, labeled "semi-vowels," shows three sounds that structural linguists usually consider half-consonant and half-vowel: /w, y, h/. If these sounds precede a vowel, they are consonants, as in the words *wet, yet,* and *hot.* When they follow a vowel, they are vowels, as in the words *how, hay,* and *yeah.* As Trager and Smith explain, the concept /y/ represents a glide of the tongue up and front, /w/ represents a glide up and back, and /h/ represents a glide toward the center of the mouth. The semivowels combine with their preceding vowel to form diphthongs.

Although theoretically any one of the three semivowels may combine with any one of the nine "pure" vowels to produce a diphthong, there are eight most widely used diphthongs in American English.

/iy/   high front vowel plus high front glide as in *team*
/tiym/

/ey/   mid front vowel plus high front glide as in *tame*
/teym/

/ay/   low central vowel plus high front glide as in *time*
/taym/

/oy/   mid back vowel plus high front glide as in *toy* /toy/

/uw/   high back vowel plus high back glide as in *too*
/tuw/

/ow/   mid back vowel plus high back glide as in *toe* /tow/

/aw/   low central vowel plus high back glide as in *towel*
/tawəl/

/eh/   mid front vowel plus centering glide as in *yeah*
/yeh/

HOW SOUNDS CONTRIBUTE TO MEANING

Sounds pronounced by speakers are not heard identically by listeners. For example, in a recording by a man whose entire tongue had been removed in a cancer operation, listeners "heard" sounds that normally require the tongue. The man communicated his meaning because the listeners automatically supplied clues from their knowledge of English sounds, morphemes, sentences, and cultural contexts. Thus they "heard" sounds that were physically impossible for the speaker to produce, and they disregarded extraneous sounds that he actually did produce.

The rhythm and music of speech—termed *intonation* by linguists—add many signals of meaning. Stress, pitch, and pause are three such signals. For example, without using stress it is impossible to pronounce the written word *convert*. As a noun, its first syllable is stressed: *CONvert*, but as a verb the stress moves to its second syllable: *conVERT*. Generally, the stressed syllable also carries a higher pitch, since stress and pitch work together to communicate meaning. With one-syllable words, the stress necessarily falls on the single syllable. However, stress can combine with pitch and pause to signal different meanings, as illustrated by the punctuations in the following examples.

Sing.   Sing?   Sing!

Phonemes form syllables and syllables form words. In words, the smallest meaningful elements are morphemes.

A morpheme is not the same as a syllable. For example, the word *babysit* has three syllables but only two morphemes. That is, the first syllable of *baby* /bey/ has no connection with a bay where boats sail, and the second syllable /biy/ does not mean a honey bee. Together, the two syllables form the smallest element of relevant meaning, "infant." Therefore the word *baby* is a morpheme. In the word *babysit*, the meaning "infant" connects properly with the meaning of the following morpheme *sit*, "to take charge of a child while the parents are away."

On the other hand, a morpheme can be less than a syllable. For example, the negative contraction *n't* added to *can* produces *can't* /kænt/, adding the meaning "negative" to *can*, but not adding a syllable. Or consider the phrase *six sheep*. The meaning "plural" is present in *sheep* but there is no added syllable to show that morpheme.

Morphemes are either bases or affixes. Most bases stand alone as words, but affixes never stand alone; they are always attached to a base—prefixes before it, suffixes after it. Affixes are either derivational or inflectional. All prefixes are derivational affixes; suffixes may be either derivational or inflectional. Derivational suffixes usually change the word's part of speech; inflectional suffixes never do. For example, the derivational suffix *–ful* changes the noun *thought* to the adjective *thoughtful*, but the inflectional suffix *–s*, added to the noun *thought*, creates *thoughts*, which is still a noun with the added meaning "plural." The absence of *–s* on *thought* is equally meaningful; it signifies "singular."

Old English had many inflectional suffixes, indicating each word's part of speech. Modern English has lost most of these suffixes, using instead word order patterns to indicate the parts of speech. The inflectional suffixes that still remain today are the following.

> Nouns: *–s* or *–es* meaning "plural"
> *–'s* or *s'* meaning "possession"
> Verbs: *–s* meaning "third person singular present tense"

—*ed* meaning "past tense" or "past participle"
—*ing* meaning "present participle"
Short adjectives: —*er* meaning "more"
—*est* meaning "most"

In English no new inflectional suffixes have been added for seven hundred years. Therefore they are a "closed class" of morphemes.

Derivational affixes—both prefixes and suffixes—are an "open class." That is, English permits new affixes to be added as needed. Recent additions are the prefixes *mini*–, *midi*–, and *maxi*–, and the suffix —*nik*. Nouns, verbs, adjectives, and adverbs all have their characteristic derivational affixes.

Noun		Verb	
—dom	dukedom	—ify	beautify
—ment	encouragement	—en	brighten
—ness	gladness	—ize	sympathize

Adjective		Adverb	
—able	reasonable	—ly	gladly
—ful	beautiful	—wise	likewise
—ic	heroic	—ways	sideways

Derivational affixes organize "word families" in English. A *word family* is a group of words related by derivation to a single base.

Noun	Verb	Adjective	Adverb
brightness	brighten	bright	brightly
beauty	beautify	beautiful	beautifully
enjoyment	enjoy	enjoyable	enjoyably
devil	bedevil	devilish	devilishly
angel		angelic	angelically
friend	befriend	friendly	
terror	terrify	{ terrible	{ terribly
		{ terrific	{ terrifically
television	televise	{ televisual	{ televisually
		{ televisional	{ televisionally

UNDERSTANDING SPELLING

Spelling is relevant chiefly to writing; obviously nobody knows how well we spell until we write. Spelling is also much more important to readers than it is to listeners. Words are easier to recognize in reading than to spell, letter by letter, in writing. Fluent readers never pay attention to each letter in each phrase of each sentence, but writers must.

History explains many of the discrepancies between English spelling and English pronunciation. The ancient Phoenicians used a writing system in which a single symbol represented a consonant plus a following vowel, with several symbols that stood for consonants alone. The Phoenicians used this system for writing their Semitic language. When the Greeks borrowed this system for writing Greek, they forced it to fit their non-Semitic language, and the correspondence between symbols and sounds became less exact. The Phoenicians had more consonant sounds than did the Greeks, and the Greeks used the extra consonant symbols for writing their vowel sounds. Thus they developed an alphabetic writing system in which each symbol (or grapheme) represented one sound (or phoneme). Later, the Romans borrowed the Greek alphabet for representing Latin phonemes, and the match grew even less precise.

Eventually, Christian missionaries brought the Roman alphabet to England and used it for writing English, a Germanic language differing from both Greek and Latin. The match between English phonemes and Roman graphemes was far from accurate. Scribes, writing manuscripts, often spelled words more or less as they pronounced them. However, when printing was invented in the fifteenth century, the spelling of words became relatively fixed. Although the "great vowel shift" later altered the pronunciation of the long stressed root vowels, English spelling was still based on the archaic pronunciation of Chaucer's Late Middle English and Shakespeare's Early Modern English. Furthermore, the earliest English books were printed by Dutch printers who often were ignorant of English pronunciation and who spelled English words by analogy with Latin roots or by other mistaken notions. Thus through a long sequence of historical accidents,

English spelling and English pronunciation have many discrepancies.

English spelling is further complicated because we have borrowed many words, called *loanwords*, from foreign languages. Every language that English has contacted in its history has loaned words to our vocabulary. Here are a few examples selected from numerous possibilities.

French: *chef, coup, potpourri*
German: *sauerkraut, edelweiss, dachshund*
Italian: *crescendo, lasagna, belladonna*
Spanish: *patio, guitar, llama*
Turkish: *caftan, khan, coffee*

Because foreign loanwords usually are spelled according to the rules of the lending language, they have to be learned as separate spelling items.

Yet in spite of its history, English spelling is essentially alphabetic; that is, graphemes usually represent phonemes systematically. Structural linguists typically use only phonemic information to set up phoneme–grapheme correspondences. For example, in 1966 Paul R. Hanna and his colleagues at Stanford University programed a computer to use only phonetic cues. In 17,009 of the most frequently used words, they determined that more than half of the consonants were spelled consistently eighty per cent of the time and that many vowels matched that level of predictability. When they programed the computer to add cues from grammar and meaning, the phoneme–grapheme correspondences became even more predictable.

Transformational–generative linguists believe that English spelling is a nearly ideal system for representing underlying relationships among words, especially the Latinate words of an educated user. To them it seems less important to record phoneme–grapheme correspondences than to record what speakers "know" about how phonemes and graphemes work together.

In other words, we control a vast store of morphophonemic information about English words and how to pronounce them. For example, we know that the plural suffix spelled –s is pronounced /s/ on *cats* but /z/ on *dogs*. We know also that the past suffix spelled –ed is pronounced /t/ on *walked*, /d/ on *warned*, and /əd/ on *wanted*. That is, we can predict the pronunciation from the phonetic environment. We automatically choose the correct phonemes to communicate the intended meaning. The spelling need not and does not reflect the pronunciation difference. However, the spelling should and usually does reflect meaningful, unpredictable contrasts between /s:z/ and /t:d/. Thus, the spellings *sip* and *zip* or *ten* and *den* reflect the underlying difference in meaning between the members of each pair of words.

In addition to such morphophonemic contrasts, English spelling graphically represents underlying root morphemes that may not be apparent in the pronunciation of the word. For example, spelling clearly records the relationship of *partial* to *part* and *partition*, in which the "silent t" is pronounced. If *partial* were spelled *parshel*, these relationships would be hidden. Spelling *sign* as *sine* would conceal its relationship to both *signify* and *signal*, in which underlying /g/ is pronounced, and would also suggest an incorrect relationship to the homonym *sine* of trigonometry.

The good speller internalizes such relationships. Teachers should foster spelling awareness in students and help them to recognize that related words are spelled alike even though they may be pronounced differently.

SUGGESTIONS FOR STUDY AND DISCUSSION

1. To deepen your appreciation for the efficiency of the alphabet, investigate the history of writing. Probably the most authoritative source of information is I. J. Gelb's *A Study of Writing*, which is most informatively illustrated.

2. Compare the pronunciation keys of several dictionaries with the Trager–Smith Phonemic Alphabet. How necessary is it for language arts students to learn the Trager–Smith Phonemic Alphabet? Why?

3. In the light of the transformational–generative tenet that the present spelling system is almost ideal for writing edu-

cated English, how would you answer a person who argued for changing English spelling to the forms suggested by the Simplified Spelling Society, as follows.

> We instinktivly shrink from eny chaenj in whot iz familyar; and whot kan be mor familyar dhan dhe form ov wurdz dhat we hav seen and riten mor tiemz dhan we kan posibly estimaet? We taek up a book printed in Amerika, and *honor* and *center* jar upon us every tiem we kum akros dhem; nae, eeven to see *forever* in plaes ov *for ever* atrakts our atenshon in an unplezant wae. But dheez ar iesolaeted kaesez; think ov dhe meny wurdz dhat wood hav to be chaenjd if eny real impruuvment wer to rezult. At dhe furst glaans a pasej in eny reformd speling looks 'kweer' or 'ugly'. Dhis objekshon iz aulwaez dhe furst to be maed; it iz purfektly natueral; it iz dhe hardest to remuuv. Indeed, its efekt iz not weekend until dhe nue speling iz noe longger nue, until it haz been seen ofen enuf to be familyar.
>
> Source: Axel Wijk, *Rules of Pronunciation for the English Language* (London: Oxford University Press, 1966), p. 152.

4. How does Shaw's suggested spelling of *ghoti* for the word *fish* show his unawareness of the importance of position in the occurrence of letters? Use the following information to help you answer.

gh as in *laugh*	o as in *women*	ti as in *nation*
Compare:	Is o pronounced /i/	Compare:
though	in any other English	*destination*
through	word?	*presentation*
dough		*plantation*

5. What evidence can you gather to support or refute the transformational–generative idea that English spelling records underlying similarities among words that may have disappeared in their pronunciation? (For example, *bomb:bombard*.)

6. How and why does the spelling and pronunciation of the negative morpheme *in–* (as in *inconsistent*) change when prefixed to *possible*, *logical*, and *relevant*? How does that knowledge aid students in spelling other words with similar beginnings?

3

Grammars

OVERVIEW AND PURPOSE OF THE CHAPTER

Children cannot learn technical grammar until they are about eleven or twelve years old because it is too abstract for the earliest stages of mental maturity. However, young children skillfully master new vocabulary when it is clearly related to an understandable context. Since normal children enter school unconsciously knowing a great deal about grammar, teachers can casually use grammatical vocabulary like *noun* and *verb* to give children names for talking about what they already know. Linguistically trained teachers can capitalize on opportunities to tap the child's built-in grammar in all subjects but especially in composition, reading, and literature. Many such opportunities should be gamelike so that learning grammar is enjoyable, not boring or confusing. Building grammatical vocabulary prepares children well for formal grammar which they will study when they develop the mental maturity to handle abstractions.

The word *grammar* has two meanings in this book. First, it means the underlying rules that speakers have intuitively grasped for comprehending and producing their language. Second, *grammar* means a written description and explanation of these rules. Full awareness of grammatical rules can help teachers and students use the system consciously and effectively.

This chapter considers the rules of standard English, that is, the kind of English used in the serious, important affairs of English-speaking people. *Webster's Third New International Dictionary* defines standard English as

> the English that with respect to spelling, grammar,
> pronunciation, and vocabulary is substantially uniform
> though not devoid of regional differences, that is
> well-established by usage in the formal and informal
> speech and writing of the educated, and that is widely recognized
> as acceptable wherever English is spoken and understood.

Since standard English is the most widespread and useful variety of English, it is the most suitable for serious study.

Within this chapter grammatical concepts that have proved useful to teachers are explained for use and reference. Indeed, the chapter is a condensed reference handbook of modern grammar. The concepts have been selected from traditional grammar, structural linguistics, transformational–generative grammar and semantics, and Firthian linguistics. The criterion for selection was the value of the ideas for classroom teachers.

Transformational–generative grammar dominates the discussion.[1] It is the most influential and useful tool for understanding the structure of English sentences and their parts. In addition, it explains many terms and concepts that teachers frequently meet in their textbooks and professional reading. Transformational theory has stimulated grammatical research in far-reaching ways. Teachers need to recognize that grammatical theory is not a finished product but an evolving exploration of knowledge about a very important human possession: language.

This chapter first discusses the basic or simplest sentences of English—their parts and how these fit together. This section draws upon traditional grammar, structural linguistics, and transformational–generative grammar. The following section then discusses transformations—both simple and complex—and how they change and combine the basic sentences to create more complicated ones.

BASIC SENTENCES

In considering what language means, we learned that certain types of words are marked as nouns, verbs, adjectives, and adverbs by derivational and inflectional affixes. Structural linguists group such words together as *form classes* because their form often shows their part of speech class. In addition, we can recognize them as nouns, verbs, adjectives, and adverbs by using context clues to help us observe how they work grammatically in sentences.

We perceive more real-world meaning in these word types than we do in words like determiners, conjunctions, and prepositions, which are not marked by characteristic affixes. The structural linguist often calls these words *function words* since they signal relationships among form classes in sentences.

All theories of grammar recognize that English sentences have two basic parts. These are called *subject* and *predicate* in traditional grammar, and *noun phrase* and *verb phrase* in transformational grammar. Transformational grammar depicts these basic sentence parts in tree diagrams, graphically displaying their underlying relationships.

SENTENCE

NOUN PHRASE	VERB PHRASE²
The chemist	danced the polka

The Noun Phrase

Traditional grammar defines a *noun* as "the name of a person, place, thing, or idea." This statement is true enough, but useless for identifying nouns. Children soon learn to use clearer grammatical signals to identify nouns. They recognize the inflections that in standard English mean "plural" and "possessive" and the derivational suffixes that mean "noun." They also recognize words like determiners and prepositions.

Determiners are of several types, and in sentences they all signal that a noun will soon appear in the sentence. Articles are the first type: *the* and *a* or *an*. *The* is the definite article; *a* and *an* are two forms of the indefinite article

THE *day is sunny.* *He bought* A *book.* *He bought* AN
orange.

Demonstratives are a second type of determiner: *this, that,
these, those.* Possessives are a third type of determiner: *my,
our, your, his, her, its, their.* The cardinal numbers, one to
ninety-nine, are a fourth type of determiner.

Like determiners, prepositions signal a "noun coming
up." Taken together, a preposition and its following noun
(called "object of the preposition") form a prepositional
phrase. A useful test for identifying prepositions is

The mouse ran ＿＿＿＿＿＿ the door.
preposition

Prepositions are words that fit into the blank, as in *The mouse
ran* TO *the door, The mouse ran* AROUND *the door, The mouse
ran* FROM *the door.* The nine most frequently used prepositions are *at, by, for, from, in, of, on, to,* and *with.*

Children also recognize personal pronouns, which can
substitute for nouns and noun phrases. For example:

(Elizabeth) was the queen.
    She
(The queen of England) greeted the ambassador.
    She

The following is the complete set of personal pronouns.

	SINGULAR		
	Subject	Object	Possessive
First person	I	me	mine
Second person	you	you	yours
Third person	he	him	his
	she	her	hers
	it	it	its
	PLURAL		
First person	we	us	ours
Second person	you	you	yours
Third person	they	them	theirs

The first person indicates the speaker, the second person indicates the person spoken to, and the third person indicates
the person or thing spoken about. The second person has
identical forms in both singular and plural.

Sentence trees show how different kinds of noun phrases are created. For example, we have seen that nouns often work with determiners, which signal when a noun is coming up. The following tree diagram shows sample noun phrases composed of determiners, and nouns.

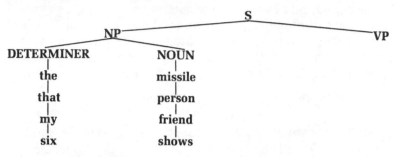

The next tree depict's a noun phrase consisting solely of a personal pronoun.

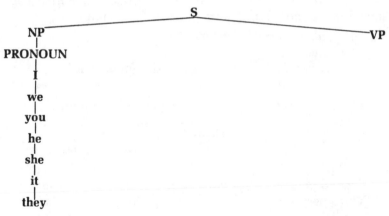

A third option for noun phrases is a proper noun. Proper nouns refer to unique individuals and items and are always capitalized in written sentences.

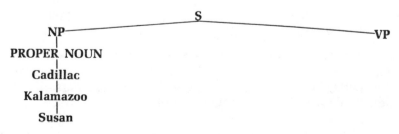

The Verb Phrase

The predicate, or verb phrase, is the second half of the English sentence. Traditional grammar defines verbs as words that "show action, being, or state of being." Again, this definition is true enough but useless for identifying verbs in sentences. As with nouns, children soon learn the inflectional and derivational affixes that mark verbs and the syntactic signals that show them in action.

In standard English two inflectional suffixes— –s and –ed—mark the tense of verbs as present or past respectively. Tense is a grammatical term meaning that an inflectional suffix appears attached to the verb stem— –s for third person singular present tense, and –ed for past tense (on regular verbs).

It is important to understand clearly that tense is not a synonym for time. Time is outside of grammar in the real world of clocks, calendars, and schedules. Often the present tense does not express present time. In Christmas comes once a year, the present comes expresses customary, repeated action, not present time. In Absence makes the heart grow fonder, the present tense makes expresses a universal truth, not present time. Present time is usually expressed by a form of be followed by a present participle, which is the verb form ending in –ing, as in She is skiing. In this sentence is carries the present tense signal, but the entire verb phrase, is skiing, communicates the meaning of present time.

For centuries English has been losing its inflectional endings and substituting phrases. Unlike Old English and Latin, Modern English is essentially a phrasal language. The verb system is an excellent example of this phrasal tendency.

One type of verbal phrase is composed of modals and the uninflected form of the main verb. Modals are a type of auxiliary verb which communicates ideas of futurity, possibility, obligation, and the like. For example, three ways to express future time are I'll agree, I will agree, and I shall agree. Will and shall are modals; I'll is a contraction for either I will or I shall. There are five modal auxiliaries in English, and four of them have past tense forms:

will: would   shall: should   may: might   can: could

The fifth modal, must, has no past tense form. Modals are the only verbal forms in English that lack the inflection –s on the third person singular of the present tense. We say, "He can go," never *"He cans go";[3] and "She may write," never *"She mays write."

English also has another set of verbal phrases, forming the so-called "perfect system." In these phrases, the verb *have* is followed by the past participle. Regular past participles carry the same past suffix –ed as the past tense does. Irregular past participles often end in –en but may have many other forms too.

> We have *stopped* our game.
> We had *broken* all records before the set ended.
> He has *made* his decision.
> The program had *begun* before the Smiths arrived.

A third set of English verbal phrases forms the so-called "progressive system." In these phrases the verb *be* is followed by the present participle, which always ends in –ing.

> We *are playing* tennis. They *were breaking* all records.

A tree diagram can illustrate all these facts about standard English verbal phrases. It needs to show that an English verb phrase has two parts: its auxiliary system and its main verb.

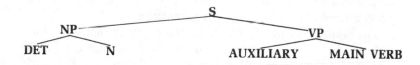

Then, one rule can summarize all the options available in the standard English auxiliary. The arrow means that the AUXILIARY, the symbol on the left, can be rewritten as the symbols on its right. (Parentheses mean that the item is optional.)

AUXILIARY —————▶ TENSE + (MODAL) +
(HAVE + PAST PARTICIPLE) +
(BE + PRESENT PARTICIPLE)

Fully translated, this rewriting rule states that the English auxiliary must show either present or past tense. No English sentence can be produced without this information. In addition, optionally, the auxiliary may have a modal, and/or *have* followed by a past participle, and/or *be* followed by a present participle.

Here is an example of the simplest tree.

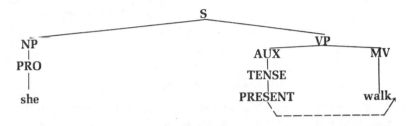

Surface sentence: *She walks.*

To produce a "real," surface–structure English sentence from this underlying grammatical information, the affix transformation is needed. Obligatory in all English sentences, it moves the inflectional suffixes to their position at the ends of the relevant words. In the above tree, the *–s* (meaning present tense) must move to the end of *walk*. The broken arrow shows the movement. The sentence surfaces as *She walks.*

In the auxiliary when a modal appears in addition to the obligatory tense, the modal occurs after the tense.

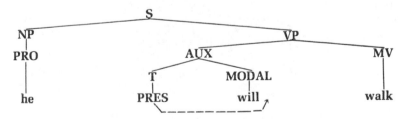

Surface sentence: *He will walk.*

No *–s* inflection surfaces because modals differ from other verbal forms and do not mark present tense third singular with this suffix.

A sentence with *have* and the past participle is illustrated by the following tree.

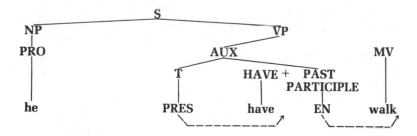

Surface sentence: *He has walked.*

To make the string of grammatical items at the bottom of the tree into a real sentence, *He has walked*, the affix transformation applies twice.

1. It moves PRES (meaning "present tense") to the right of *have* to create *has*.
2. It moves EN (meaning "past participle") to the right of *walk*, creating *walked*.

The final auxiliary option, *be* followed by the present participle ending in *–ing*, is illustrated by the following tree.

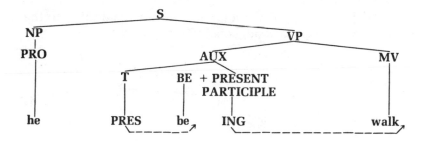

Surface sentence: *He is walking.*

The affix transformation, again applying twice, moves the tense suffix to the right of *be*, surfacing as the irregular form *is*, and the ING (meaning "present participle") to the right of the main verb *walk* to create *walking*.

Sentences may use any combination of the various auxiliary options. The following tree illustrates using all the available options simultaneously.

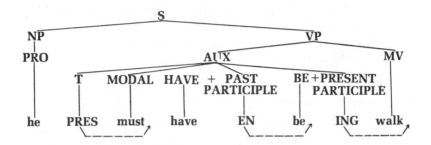

Surface sentence: *He must have been walking.*

The affix transformation, applying three times, moves the tense suffix to the right of the modal *must*, which surfaces as the uninflected form *must*, since modals lack the third person present tense suffix –*s*. The affix transformation also moves the EN (meaning "past participle") to the right of *be*, surfacing as the form *been*, and the ING (meaning "present participle") to the right of the main verb *walk* to create *walking*.

The uninflected verb form is called the *infinitive*; it is often preceded by *to* (*he wanted to walk*), which then is not a preposition but a verb marker. If we know the five essential parts of an English verb, we are prepared to use it in any context. (Only *be* has more than five essential parts.) These five essential parts are

1. the infinitive,
2. the third person singular of the present tense,
3. the past tense,
4. the past participle,
5. the present participle.

All these parts have been illustrated in the preceding tree diagrams.

Most English verbs are regular: their infinitive supplies all essential information about their various parts. The third person singular present adds –*s* to the infinitive, the past tense and past participle add –*ed* or –*d* to it, and the present participle adds –ing to it. Relatively few irregular verbs have survived from Old English, resisting the pull of the regular pattern. All new verbs entering the language automatically adopt the regular form. Most of the surviving irregular verbs are used very frequently, such as *be, have, do,* and *go.* Children learn their forms because they hear them so often. However, irregular verb forms are indicators of standard usage, and teachers should help students learn them.

There are three principal types of English verbs: intransitive, transitive, and linking. Tree diagrams show their differences clearly. The first tree shows an intransitive verb, which can be recognized by the absence of a noun phrase after it. The main verb can stand as the last word in the sentence.

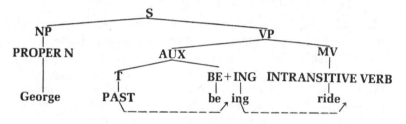

Surface sentence: *George was riding.*

On the other hand, a transitive verb must be followed by a noun phrase to complete its meaning. This noun phrase is called its *direct object.* It has a different referent from that of the first noun phrase in the sentence, which is the subject.

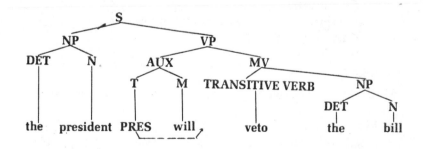

Surface sentence: *The president will veto the bill.*

The third class of main verbs is linking verbs. They may be followed by either a noun phrase or an adjective. In either case the meaning of the noun or adjective links back to the subject noun phrase in the sentence. In the following examples *lieutenant* refers to *his uncle,* just as *nervous* describes *his uncle* after the linking verb *become.* Such nouns and adjectives are called *predicate nouns* and *predicate adjectives* respectively.

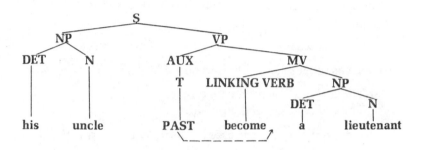

Surface sentence: *His uncle became a lieutenant.*

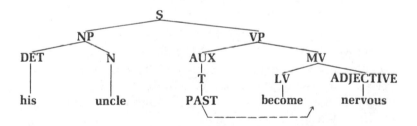

Surface sentence: *His uncle became nervous.*

Here is a summary of the absence or presence of noun phrases after the three main types of English verbs.

1. Intransitive verbs are not followed by a noun phrase.
2. Transitive verbs are followed by noun phrases different in reference from their subject noun phrase.
3. Linking verbs are followed by noun phrases identical in reference with their subject noun phrases.

Many verbs serve as more than one type of verb, depending on the structure of the sentence. Note the verb *turn*.

> Intransitive: The earth turns.
> Transitive: Bill turned the page.
> Linking: The milk turned sour.

Adjectives

Adjectives can often be identified by the test frame:

> The _____ NOUN seemed very _____
>   ADJECTIVE   ADJECTIVE

Adjectives must fit sensibly into both blanks.

> The *tall* man seemed very *tall*.
> The *old* coat seemed very *old*.

For example, in the phrases *the biology professor*, *the singing waiter*, and the *dedicated building*, the test frame reveals that the modifiers are not adjectives.

> • The biology professor seemed very biology.
> • The singing waiter seemed very singing.
> • The dedicated building seemed very dedicated.

Such modifiers are usually nouns or verbs as shown by their inflectional markers. Nouns which modify nouns are called *noun adjuncts*, and verbs which modify nouns are usually present or past participles. As will be noted later in the chapter, adjectivalization transformations can explain these modification structures.

The word *very* in the test frame belongs to a special group of adverbs often called *intensifiers*. These adverbs work with adjectives and manner adverbs, but not with verbs. Consider the following examples.

> She is *very* intelligent. Intensifier with adjective.
> She spoke *very* firmly. Intensifier with manner adverb.
> • She *very* walked. Intensifier with verb.

Other frequently used intensifiers are *rather*, *somewhat*, and *quite*.

Adjectives can also be identified by their optional inflections, –er and –est, or by the words *more* and *most*, indicating comparison. One- or two-syllable adjectives can use –er and –est; longer adjectives use more and most.

> *Jerry is smart. John is smarter. Joe is smartest.*
> *Smith is conservative. Jones is more conservative. Green is most conservative.*

Adverbs

Any English sentence can end with an adverb phrase which adds details of time, place, manner, and many other meanings. Adverb phrases may surface as single-word adverbs (like *yesterday, outside, quickly*), as adverbial phrases with or without a preposition (like *yesterday afternoon, at home, in this way*), or as adverbialization transforms, composed of a subordinator plus a sentence (like *after the train left, because the rain fell, although winter was over*). Here we discuss single-word adverbs and adverbial phrases, prepositional and otherwise. We postpone adverbialization transforms to the section on complex transformations.

The following tree shows an adverb phrase as the rightmost branch of a sentence.

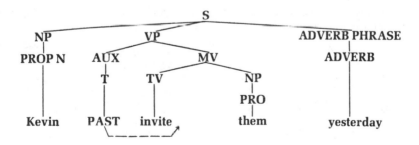

Surface sentence: *Kevin invited them yesterday.*

Several adverb phrases may occur in the same sentence, and they may occur as part of the verb phrase as well as part of the main sentence. As part of the verb phrase, they are verb modifiers and are not movable; as part of the main sentence, they are sentence modifiers and are usually movable.

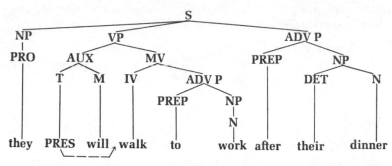

Surface sentence: *They will walk to work after their dinner.*

SIMPLE TRANSFORMATIONS

We have been examining the simplest basic sentences, consisting of one NP and one VP (and possibly one ADVP). Sentences as simple as these are relatively rare, but all complicated sentences are essentially variations and combinations of these. Transformations explain how underlying patterns relate to actual spoken or written sentences.

Sentences affected by transformations are called transforms. For example, every sentence has its negative transform, signaled by *not* or *n't*.

His plane is landing. ──────→ His plane is not (or isn't) landing.

Every statement also has question transforms, signaled by the inversion of the subject NP and the first element of the AUX.

His plane is landing. ──────→ Is his plane landing?

Such questions ask for a *Yes* or *No* answer. Other questions ask for more information; they are marked by WH–words: *who (whose, whom), what, which, when, where, why, how.*

His plane is landing. ──────→ Which plane is landing?

Negative and question transformations automatically involve the "empty do" transformation. Consider these sentences:

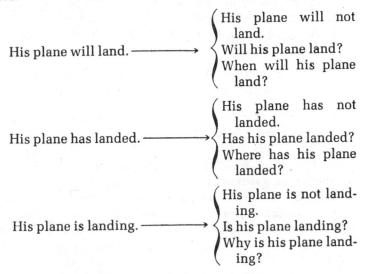

His plane will land. ⟶ {
His plane will not land.
Will his plane land?
When will his plane land?
}

His plane has landed. ⟶ {
His plane has not landed.
Has his plane landed?
Where has his plane landed?
}

His plane is landing. ⟶ {
His plane is not landing.
Is his plane landing?
Why is his plane landing?
}

In these examples, the AUX contains a modal, HAVE + EN, or BE + ING to carry the tense signal in the transform. However, in sentences without one of these options, English provides an "empty" do, does, or did to perform this function, as in:

His plane lands. ⟶ {
His plane does not land.
Does his plane land?
When does his plane land?
}

These forms of do have no built-in meaning in such transforms; they are merely carriers for the obligatory tense signal of the AUX.

Other simple transformations are more limited in their occurrence than negatives and questions, which can apply to any sentence in the language. For example, the imperative transformation cannot work without you as subject NP in the underlying structure. In other words, in the imperative Come in, a you is understood as being the subject of Come in (You come in) even though it does not appear in the transform.

Some transformations present stylistic options to English users, offering them more than one way to state the same idea.

One such is the *"there" transformation*. It applies to sentences that have

1. An indefinite determiner in the subject NP,
2. A form of *be* in the VP, either as AUX or MV,
3. An adverb phrase of place if the *be* is the main verb of the sentence.

An example is *An ant*   *There is an ant*
is in the sugar. ⟶ *in the sugar.*

In such sentences the subject moves after the first element of the VP, and the subject NP position is filled by the expletive *there*. This *there* is not an adverb. It is a place holder in the subject position, which in English must be filled; it cannot be left empty, as it can in Spanish, for example.

Another stylistic option is the *passive transformation*. Any transitive verb can be passivized. For example, *Helen will write the note* can be passivized to *The note will be written by Helen*. In the passive transform the subject and direct object NP's switch places, *be* and *by* are added, and the main verb changes to the past participle form *(written)*.

The *adverb movement transformation* also presents stylistic options. The adverb phrase often may move from its position at the end of the sentence to other locations. For example, in the sentence *Kevin met her yesterday*, the adverb of time *yesterday* may move to the front of the sentence: *Yesterday Kevin met her at the bank*. In the sentence *They will walk to work after their dinner*, the adverbial phrase *after their dinner* may move to the front of the sentence, but the adverbial phrase *to work* may not move because it modifies the verb *walk* rather than the entire sentence. It is locked into the verb phrase.

Another movement transformation is the *verb particle transformation*. It can occur with certain two-word transitive verbs like *talk over* meaning "discuss," *call up* meaning "phone," and *throw out* meaning "discard." In it, the direct object moves between the verb and the particle.

The fans talked   The fans talked
over the game. ⟶ the game over.

Rhoda called up   Rhoda called
Brenda. ⟶ Brenda up.

We threw out   We threw the
the records. ⟶ records out.

Note that when the direct object NP is a pronoun, the two parts of the verb *must* be separated.

The fans talked *it* over.
Rhoda called *her* up.
We threw *them* out.

Understanding simple transformations like the *there*, passive, adverb movement, and verb particle transformations helps students become aware of the options they have in creating sentences. Recognizing available choices enhances students' skill in using their English grammar.

COMPLEX TRANSFORMATIONS

We have examined basic sentences and simple transformations. We will now consider complex transformations, which explain how simple sentences become complicated. Essentially, complex transformations involve the processes of joining or insertion.

Joining

Two or more sentences may be combined by the use of conjunctions like *and, but, (either)* . . . *or, neither* . . . *nor,* or *whether* . . . *or.*

Gregg barbecued the steak and Francine made the drinks.
The singers rehearsed but the dancers slept.

Whenever parts of the joined sentences are repeated, the conjunction may erase and substitute for this duplication, joining parallel grammatical items.

Jones will win the election. + McGinty will win the election. = (Either) Jones or McGinty will win the election.

The road was narrow. + The road was dusty. = The road was narrow and dusty.

Grandmother smiled bravely. + Grandmother smiled steadily. = Grandmother smiled bravely and steadily.

There were wrinkles beside his eyes. + There were wrinkles around his mouth. = There were wrinkles beside his eyes and around his mouth.

Any number of items may be joined, limited only by good sense. In the following sentence, for example, six nouns join in a series; commas replace the *and*'s before all but the last noun. (The comma before the *and* is optional before the final member of a series.)

We bought bread, butter, jelly, ham, salami, and cheese.

The sentence represents the joining of six basic sentences:

We bought bread.	We bought butter.	We bought jelly.
We bought ham.	We bought salami.	We bought cheese.

When the repetition is of the noun, instead of *and*, we may use *who* or *which*, depending on whether or not the noun is a person. In such cases, the construction is punctuated by a comma and called a *nonrestrictive construction*. This situation will be discussed further under adjectivalization.

I know Joshua Davis. + Joshua Davis is a famous lawyer.

I know Joshua Davis, and he is a famous lawyer.

or

I know Joshua Davis, who is a famous lawyer.

Insertion

Sentences can also be combined by inserting or embedding one into another. The inserted sentence is called the *insert*, and the receiving sentence is called the *receiver*. The three main types of insertions are:

1. nominalization, which explains how a sentence to be inserted can be transformed into a noun-like insert to function as a noun in its receiver—as subject, direct object, predicate noun, or object of a preposition;

2. adjectivalization, which explains how a sentence to be inserted can be transformed into an adjective-like insert to function as a modifier of a noun in its receiver;

3. adverbialization, which explains how a sentence to be inserted can be transformed into an adverb-like insert to function as an adverb in its receiver.

The next three sections discuss each insertion type in detail.

Nominalization. All sentences can be transformed into noun-like (or nominal) inserts and then inserted into receivers to work like nouns. There are five forms of nominal inserts, but not all forms work in all receivers. In each of the following examples, the empty box is a placeholder showing where the receiver can accept the nominal insert.

1. *That + Sentence.* In these nominal inserts, the word *that* precedes the insert sentence.

As subject:

> Receiver: ☐ is interesting
> Insert: Pablo speaks English
> Result: *That Pablo speaks English* is interesting.

As direct object:

> Receiver: I know ☐
> Insert: Judy is going to New York
> Result: I know *that Judy is going to New York.*

As predicate noun:

> Receiver: My idea is ☐
> Insert: The price is too high
> Result: My idea is *that the price is too high.*

In the direct object and predicate nominative examples above, the word *that* is optional. The meaning is clear without its presence in the result sentence.

2. *WH–word Sentence.* In these nominal inserts, WH–words substitute in the receiver for indefinites such as *something,*

somewhere, sometime, and *somehow.* wh–words always move to the front of their inserts.

As subject:

> Receiver: [＿＿＿＿＿] was interesting
> Insert: Lucy said something
> Result: *What Lucy said* was interesting.

As direct object:

> Receiver: I know [＿＿＿＿＿]
> Insert: Laura went somewhere
> Result: I know *where Laura went.*

As predicate noun:

> Receiver: My question is [＿＿＿＿＿]
> Insert: Lilian went sometime
> Result: My question is *when Lilian went.*

As object of a preposition:

> Receiver: We are interested in [＿＿＿＿＿]
> Insert: Lucy went somehow
> Result: We are interested in *how Lucy went.*

3. *Infinitive.* As you recall, an *infinitive* is the plain, uninflected form of the verb. As nominal inserts, infinitives are usually preceded by their marker *to* (or *for* . . . *to,* or wh– word + *to*). The insert verb loses its inflections and, if its subject is indefinite or duplicates the subject of the receiver, that subject disappears in the result.

As subject:

> Receiver: [＿＿＿＿＿] is interesting
> Insert: Someone skis
> Result: *To ski* is interesting.

> Receiver: [＿＿＿＿＿] is interesting
> Insert: Karl skis
> Result: *For Karl to ski* is interesting.

> Receiver: [＿＿＿＿＿] is interesting
> Insert: Someone skis somehow
> Result: *How to ski* is interesting.

As predicate noun:

> Receiver: Her desire is [＿＿＿＿＿]
> Insert: She skis
> Result: Her desire is *to ski.*

As direct object:

> Receiver: Her associates wanted [＿＿＿＿＿]
> Insert: Her associates skied
> Result: Her associates wanted *to ski.*

> Receiver: Her associates wanted [＿＿＿＿＿]
> Insert: She skied
> Result: Her associates wanted *her to ski.*

> Receiver: Her associates asked [＿＿＿＿＿]
> Insert: Someone skied somewhere
> Result: Her associates asked *where to ski.*

4. Gerund. These nominal inserts end in –ing. In traditional grammar, gerunds are called "verbal nouns," highlighting the fact that they are verbal in inserts but noun-like in receivers.

As subject:

> Receiver: [＿＿＿＿＿] was delightful
> Insert: Someone danced
> Result: *Dancing* was delightful.

As direct object:

> Receiver: We like [＿＿＿＿＿]
> Insert: We dance
> Result: We like *dancing.*

As predicate noun:

> Receiver: Happiness is [＿＿＿＿＿]
> Insert: Someone dances
> Result: Happiness is *dancing.*

As object of preposition:

> Receiver: They are interested in [＿＿＿＿＿]
> Insert: She dances
> Result: They are interested in *her dancing.*

5. *Cognate nouns.* Many verbs have related nouns which are alternatives to their gerunds.

As subject:

> Receiver: [   ] was charming
> Insert: She accepted
> Result: *Her acceptance* was charming.

> Receiver: [   ] was welcome
> Insert: The plane arrived
> Result: *The plane's arrival* was welcome.

As direct object:

> Receiver: We loved [   ]
> Insert: They explained
> Result: We loved *their explanation.*

As predicate noun:

> Receiver: The problem is [   ]
> Insert: She confessed
> Result: The problem is *her confession.*

As object of preposition:

> Receiver: Joan asked about [   ]
> Insert: Tom refused
> Result: Joan asked about *Tom's refusal.*

Adjectivalization. Adjectivalization explains how prenoun and postnoun modifiers get into sentences. When two sentences both contain a noun with the same referent, adjectivalization may take place. In such cases a *relative* may substitute for the shared noun in the insert. The relatives are *who (whose, whom), which,* and *that.* An adjectival insert introduced by a relative is called a *relative clause.* A relative clause modifies its shared noun in the receiver.[4]

> Receiver: The detective hurried to the scene
> Insert: The detective heard the alarm
> Result: The detective who (or that) heard the alarm hurried to the scene.

Receiver: He bought the shoes
Insert: The shoes were cheap
Result: He bought the shoes which (or that) were cheap.

The process of adjectivalization can be illustrated graphically by simplified tree diagrams, which show the relationship between the receiver and the insert. For instance, the two examples given above can be illustrated as follows:

Receiver: The detective *Insert* hurried to the scene

The detective heard the alarm

Receiver: He bought the shoes *Insert*

The shoes were cheap

Any noun can be modified by an insert sentence. Modification of nouns is the basic nature of adjectives and adjectivalizations. After insertion, the inserts often may be reduced by the deletion of words which are not necessary to the sense of the result sentence. If an insert is reduced to one word, it usually moves in front of the noun it modifies.

For example, here are several pairs of surface sentences that have the same meaning even though one has been shortened by the deletion of unnecessary words. One tree underlies both surface results.

Receiver: The steak *Insert* was delicious

We bought the steak

Results: The steak that we bought was delicious.
or
The steak we bought was delicious.

Receiver: He bought the shoes *Insert*

The shoes were cheap

Results: He bought the shoes that were cheap.
or
He bought the cheap shoes.

Receiver: Dick sat on the tack *Insert*

The tack was brass

Results: Dick sat on the tack that was brass.
or
Dick sat on the brass tack.

Receiver: He smiled at the girl *Insert*

The girl was waving at him

Results: He smiled at the girl who was waving at him.
or
He smiled at the girl waving at him.

Receiver: He counted the change *Insert*

The change was returned by the cashier

Results: He counted the change which was returned by
the cashier.
or
He counted the change returned by the cashier.

Receiver: He is reading the book Insert

The book has been censored

Results: He is reading the book which has been censored.

or

He is reading the censored book.

You may have noticed that none of the above adjectival inserts is punctuated by commas. If any were, they would be nonrestrictive constructions. The comma punctuation correlates in speech with certain intonation signals: strong stress, pause, and slight drop in pitch. Try saying and listening to the following sentences so that you "hear the commas."

> We arrived on Wednesday, which was a beautiful day.
> He played paddle tennis with Jennie Stuart, who was a real estate broker.
> Or in a shortened form: He played paddle tennis with Jennie Stuart, a real estate broker.

In such sentences, the nonrestrictive construction clearly shows that the inserts add information which is different from the main focus of the receiver sentence. In other words, the relationship is more one of joining sentences than of inserting one into the other. In speaking, nonrestrictive constructions occur most often at the end of receiver sentences. In writing, nonrestrictive constructions often occur internally, framed by commas. These signal that the insert interrupts the receiver and adds information. The main focus of the receiver is outside the commas. Notice how the absence of commas in the following sentences expands the main focus of the receiver by including all the information in the receiver sentences.

> The detective who was a lawyer hurried to the scene.
> The project which (or that) was funded by the United States government began last April.
> The books which (or that) had been banned caused a lot of trouble.

Adverbialization. The third type of insertion transformation is adverbialization, in which an insert sentence enters a receiver sentence to work adverbially. That is, these inserts modify verbs, adjectives, adverbs, or the entire sentence. Adverbial inserts that modify the entire sentence can usually move around rather freely in receivers if the speaker or writer so desires.

Adverbial inserts are marked in the surface structure by function words called *subordinators* or *includers*. Here is a fairly complete list of subordinators.

SUBORDINATOR	MEANING	EXAMPLE
where	Place	She will stay where she is happy.
when, while, after, before, until, till, since, as soon as	Time	When the wagon broke, Ray fell out.
as if, like	Manner	He smiles as if he is pleased.
because, since, as, so that, in order that	Cause (reason, purpose)	He laughed because he won.
though, although, even though	Concession	Although it rained, we had the picnic.
if, unless, whether . . . or not	Condition	If we go early, we can see everything.
as . . . as, –er than,	Comparison	She is as kind as her mother.
more . . . than,		He ran faster than her sister. She ran more quickly than her cousin.
less . . . than		He is smarter than his brother. She is more interesting than her cousin.
so . . . that, such that	Result	The sun was so bright that she got a bad sunburn.

Adverbialization can be illustrated by a simplified tree diagram.

Receiver: She will stay *Insert*

(where) she is happy

Result: She will stay where she is happy.

Receiver: She is kind *Insert*

(as . . . as) her mother is kind

Result: She is as kind as her mother.

(Note that the second *is kind* is duplication and can therefore be deleted without loss of meaning. The first *as* moves into surface position before *kind* in the receiver.)

Receiver: She ran quickly *Insert*

(more . . . than) her cousin ran quickly

Result: She ran more quickly than her cousin.

(Again the duplication disappears in the result sentence without loss of meaning. The *more* moves into its surface position before the *quickly* in the receiver.) Neither of the last two adverbial inserts is movable. Both are locked into their modification position close to the adjective *(kind)* and the adverb *(quickly)* which they modify.

SUGGESTIONS FOR STUDY AND DISCUSSION

1. Collect other definitions of standard English to compare with the definition of *Webster's Third New International Dictionary*. Possible sources: Robbins Burling, *English in Black and White*, pp. 24–27; Virginia F. Allen, "Teaching Standard English as a Second Dialect," pp. 238–243 and David De-Camp, "Dimensions of English Usage," pp. 200–215, both in *Contemporary English: Change and Variation*, ed. David L. Shores.

2. Check other textbooks to compare their handling of the concepts presented in this chapter. Some possibilities are: Jeanne H. Herndon, *A Survey of Modern Grammars*; J. N. Hook and Michael G. Crowell, *Modern English Grammar for Teachers*; and Owen Thomas and Eugene R. Kintgen, *Transformational Grammar and the Teacher of English: Theory and Practice.*

3. In Shakespeare's time, the "empty do" transformation was just becoming common in English. He could acceptably produce negatives and questions with or without it. Check any of his writing's to see how frequently he chose one or the other. Does the age of the speaker have anything to do with his choice, as far as you can discover?

4. Examine the language games discussed by James Moffett in *A Student-Centered Language Arts Curriculum, Grades K–13: A Handbook for Teachers*, and by Abraham B. Hurwitz and Arthur Goddard in *Games to Improve Your Child's English*. Which ones could you use?

5. Compare tree diagrams with any other system of sentence diagraming you may have learned previously. What advantages or disadvantages do trees have?

6. Not all two-word verbs in English can undergo the verb particle transformation. Consider, for example, *go over* ("review"), *keep on* ("continue"), *run over* ("hit by a car"), *look out* ("beware"), *look like* ("resemble"), *run into* ("meet by chance"). What generalizations can you make about two-word verbs in English?

7. In this chapter each transformation has been discussed separately. However, in actual use, any sentence may contain several transformations simultaneously. How many of the simple transformations can you apply simultaneously to the following sentences?

    a. He wanted a guppy.
    b. A stone was in her shoe.
    c. You will enter the race.
    d. Snow was all over the road.
    e. Our poodle caught a rabbit yesterday.

NOTES

¹ Many other grammatical analyses are available: Fillmore's case grammar, Lamb's stratificational grammar, Halliday's scale and category grammar, Chafe's semantically oriented grammar, Pike's tagmemics, and others.

² In tree diagrams, after the term has been spelled out in capital letters, it is subsequently abbreviated: SENTENCE, S; NOUN PHRASE, NP; VERB PHRASE, VP.

³ An asterisk (*) in front of an example indicates that the example is not acceptable in normal English.

⁴ This type of insertion is also called relativization instead of adjectivalization because, in transformational theory, the relative clause is the starting point of the insertion.

4

The Historical Development of English

OVERVIEW AND PURPOSE OF THE CHAPTER

Language changes as time passes. Usually this change is gradual, although new words may enter the language suddenly just as the verb *softland* did when a man first stepped on the moon. The schools are a conservative force that retards, but cannot prevent, language variation. The awareness by teachers that change is normal and inevitable can enlighten all aspects of their instruction.

Three factors explain language change. The first is normal variation, which occurs as new ideas and inventions develop and enter into language. The second factor is geographic change. Whenever people move to a new location, their language changes as it adapts to new situations. The third factor is the importation of foreign words and expressions. When languages meet, their speakers and writers exchange words, thereby enriching both languages.

The historical development of English is a progression from Anglo–Saxon to Modern English. For discussion purposes, linguists usually divide this spectrum into three periods: Old English from our earliest records in the seventh century to about 1100 A.D.; Middle English from about 1100 to about 1500; and Modern English from about 1500 to the present.

The prehistoric people of the British Isles spoke a Celtic language; variations still survive in Scotland, Wales, and Ireland. Although in the fifth and sixth centuries Britain was invaded from the mainland by Angles, Saxons, and Jutes, the earliest surviving records of our ancient written language date from after 600 when Roman missionaries converted the Anglo-Saxons to Christianity and taught them the Latin alphabet. Then in the ninth century Britain was invaded by the Norsemen, whose language left traces on Old English. From William the Conqueror's conquest of England in 1066 and until the end of the Hundred Years' War in 1453, Norman French greatly influenced the English language. As William imported it along with his followers from Normandy, it was the language of the court and was spoken by the nobility.

Later, variations in English had causes other than invasion. British trade, exploration, and colonization spread English throughout the world, and new words were adopted from the contacted peoples. In 1476 Caxton introduced the printing press to England; the printed page made more available expanded the reading public. With the beginning of the Industrial Revolution in the mid-eighteenth century, new commercial and industrial words were added and a newly rich class emerged who wanted their English usage to match that of their social "betters." English grammars appeared to meet their need for "rules of correctness." In 1755 Dr. Samuel Johnson's dictionary was published and subsequently was naïvely used as a guide to "correct English grammar." As the British Empire grew, English was used as a second language in India and also in many African countries, where no single universal native language existed. Thus various world dialects of English have been developed.

This unbroken history of change continues. Teachers need to be aware of linguistic change so that they can expect their students' language to differ from their own. Differences can stimulate interesting class discussions, especially in the analysis of older literature. Teachers can anticipate students' unfamiliarity with words that were once common but are rarely used today. In dictionary study, obsolete and archaic words testify to language change and, when students meet them in reading older literature, provide stimulating opportunities for discussing the permanence of change.

Changes occur in four main areas of language: pronunciation, word forms, sentence structure, and vocabulary. We will discuss each in turn.

CHANGES IN PRONUNCIATION

Sound spectrograms—visible pictures of speech made in speech laboratories—reveal that no two sounds are ever pronounced identically. Although individual differences seem too small to be significant, through the centuries they accumulate until eventually observable differences can be noted. It is partly on the basis of such accumulated differences that linguists separate Old English from Middle English, and Middle English from Modern English.

For example, in the course of history certain consonant clusters have changed in pronunciation in a word. The k of *knob, knot,* and *know* and the t of *listen* and *glisten* were formerly pronounced as /k/ and /t/ respectively, but they are "silent" in Modern English.

Vowels have also changed in pronunciation. Between the fourteenth and the sixteenth century, the Great Vowel Shift occurred in English. All the long stressed root vowels changed in pronunciation. The low and mid vowels moved upward; the highest vowels moved downward and acquired front or back off-glides, becoming diphthongs. This shift occurred after printing had more or less frozen English spelling, which did not change to reflect the new pronunciation of the vowels. No one understands why this vowel shift happened in English and not in the continental European languages, but, as a result, English is more difficult to spell than Spanish, Italian, or some other European languages.

CHANGES IN WORD FORMS

Like all languages, English has its own individual patterns that new words entering the language must follow. The characteristic prefixes and derivational suffixes will be used to form new words. For example, in 1949 *Webster's New International Dictionary*, 2nd edition, recorded the trademark *Escalator*, meaning "a stairway or incline arranged like an endless belt so that the steps or treads ascend or descend continuously." This edition also stated that the noun *escalator* (without the capital *E*) meant "such a stairway or incline," and that the verb *escalate* (either transitive or intransitive) meant "To ascend by or as by escalator." *Webster's Third New International Dictionary*, published in 1961, shows that *escalator* had greatly widened in meaning as a noun and also had become an "adjective" as in *escalator clause*,[1] and a new noun had entered the *escalator* family: *escalation*. Between 1966 and 1971, the verb *deescalate* appeared, forming a new word with an opposite meaning from *escalate:* "To decrease in extent, volume, number, amount, or scope." This verb also brought its family into the language: *deescalation*, *deescalator*, and *deescalatory*, all built by regular English derivational suffixes.

Regular patterns are very powerful in forcing irregular patterns out of the language. For example, the old irregular plural form of *brother*, *brethren*, has been replaced by the regular *brothers*, except in some sermons and prayers. Of the hundreds of irregular verbs in Old English only about 150 remain. The others have been pulled into the regular pattern. Old English regularly made manner adverbs by adding –e to adjectives. Today, the regular manner adverb suffix is –ly, and so we would automatically invent *deescalatorily*, if we needed an adverb for the *deescalate* family.

Such changes in word form are frequent and explain why dictionaries need to be constantly updated.

CHANGES IN SENTENCE STRUCTURE

The arrangement of words in sentences is more important today than it was in Old English. In that period words had many inflectional suffixes that showed how they fitted together to communicate the intended meaning of the sentences. Today most of these inflectional suffixes have disappeared, and therefore word order is crucial in sentences. The normal word order of the present-day English statement is the subject, followed by the verb with its object or completer if there is one. For example, *Kevin kicked the horse* and *The horse kicked Kevin* have different meanings, but the only signal to that fact is the word order. This knowledge should alert teachers to comprehension problems that their students may experience when poets, for example, violate normal word order.

The loss of inflections has also resulted in the tendency to use phrases rather than possessives. Thus we tend to say, "the bulbs of the chandelier" rather than "the chandelier's bulbs," and "the corner of the bay" rather than "the bay's corner."

We have already discussed the fact that between the time of Shakespeare and the present, the "do" transformation has become indispensable in negatives and questions when no other AUX form is present to carry the tense signal.

Teachers may observe other distinctive differences between their students' sentence structure and their own. Such differences can furnish interesting topics for class discussion. Innovations should be expected, as English continues its development in the mouths of its speakers.

CHANGES IN VOCABULARY

Throughout its history, English has constantly borrowed words from other languages (as mentioned in chapter 2). These loanwords not only have enriched our vocabulary but also have become so much a part of ordinary speech that only a student of language history is usually conscious of their foreign origin.

Other modifications in vocabulary involve changes in word meanings. As words are used, their meanings may improve or worsen, narrow or widen.

For example, *knight* used to mean servant but now has been elevated to mean a man specially honored by the ruler of

England. *Governor* formerly meant head officer of a prison but today has increased in status to mean the top executive of a state in the United States. Contrariwise, other words have acquired less favorable meanings. *Boor* used to mean peasant, while *censure* meant opinion. Neither had negative connotations, as they have today; both were neutral in meaning.

Other words have narrowed in meaning. *Meat* used to mean food; *hound*, any kind of dog; *deer*, any kind of animal. Still other words have widened in meaning. *Mill* once meant a place for grinding meal or flour. In fact, *mill* and *meal* are historically related. Today there are steel mills and woolen mills as well as grain mills. *Barn* used to mean a storehouse for barley; today it has widened to mean a storehouse for any kind of grain as well as a building to house livestock.

These examples are part of the history of language and undoubtedly change will continue to occur in the future. We cannot predict what these changes will be, but we do know that they will take place. Changes cease only when a language is no longer spoken, that is, when it becomes a "dead language." This fact helps teachers adopt an inquiring and perceptive point of view that makes their teaching both more informed and more rewarding.

SUGGESTIONS FOR DISCUSSION AND STUDY

1. For a clear, interesting overview of the history of the English language, listen to and discuss the recording *Our Changing Language*, side 1, by Evelyn Gott Burack and Raven I. McDavid, Jr., which is distributed by the National Council of Teachers of English. It contains excerpts from *Beowulf*, Chaucer's *Canterbury Tales*, and Shakespeare.

2. For a graphic view of the development of the English language, examine the portfolio of "Leaflets on Historical Linguistics," published by the National Council of Teachers of English. It offers six leaflets ranging from *Beowulf* (1000 A.D.) through *The Peterborough Chronicle* (1140), Chaucer (1410), Caxton (1490), Shakespeare (1604), and Pope (1732). Each leaflet contains an introduction placing the text in its historical context, a photo facsimile from the original manuscript

(with a transcription or translation if necessary), and finally, exercises for study. The exercises concern four important areas of language change: vocabulary, grammar, pronunciation, and graphics.

3. Familiarize yourself with the *Oxford English Dictionary* (OED)—the greatest dictionary of the English language built on historical principles. The Preface states: "The aim of this Dictionary is to present in alphabetic series the words that have formed the English vocabulary from the earliest records to the present day." (That is, to the date of its publication, 1884 to 1928.) Its original thirteen volumes were reproduced micrographically and published in two volumes in 1971.

4. Slang, which gains and loses popularity very quickly, is a speeded-up example of language change. Discuss the truth of this statement in the light of your own experience. How might a study of slang be used in language arts teaching to reinforce students' sense of language change?

5. Study the origins of English words in *A History of Foreign Words in English* by Mary S. Serjeantson. This interesting book organizes English loanwords by their geographic sources.

6. Many words and expressions have an amusing history. Investigate some of them in books such as Wilfred Funk's *Word Origins and Their Romantic Stories*; Charles Earle Funk's books *A Hog on Ice and Other Curious Expressions, Thereby Hangs a Tale: Stories of Curious Word Origins, Horsefeathers and Other Curious Words*; and Bergen Evans' *Comfortable Words*.

NOTES

[1] We would term *escalator* a "noun adjunct"—a noun modifying a noun by adjectivalization insertion.

5

Dialects, Dictionaries, and Usage

OVERVIEW AND PURPOSE OF THE CHAPTER

We may sunbathe in bikinis and graduate in caps and gowns, but we would never reverse our use of these outfits. In other words, clothing is expected to be appropriate to the occasion of use. The same criterion holds for language. We would never say to a second grader, "Appropriate language usage depends on several interlocking factors composing the total communication situation." The child would be completely mystified by the inappropriate, big words. Long experience has taught teachers to choose language suited to the context in which it is used. However, students need help in learning how to do this.

Linguistically informed teachers realize that there is always more than one way to express any idea, although some ways are more appropriate than others in a given situation. The idea that there is one and only one "correct" way to express an idea is both linguistically naïve and counterproductive in classrooms. The wise language arts teacher encourages students to observe usage variety in literature and to experiment with language choices in their composition work.

In evaluating current English usage, at least seven interlocking viewpoints are relevant. The first viewpoint is socioeconomic-educational and concerns the spectrum of usage extending from standard to nonstandard English. It reflects the speakers' socioeconomic status and/or education. The second viewpoint is stylistic. Formal ceremonies like baptisms and funerals require usage quite distinct from that of informal notes or slangy remarks to intimate friends. The third viewpoint is sex-based and exhibits a spectrum of usage extending from the mild, gentle words considered to be extremely feminine to the obscenities considered rough and masculine. The fourth viewpoint is methodological—the choice between speech and writing. We do not speak as we write, nor write as we speak. Each method of communication has its own signals: speech has intonation; writing has spelling, punctuation, and capitalization. The fifth viewpoint is historical, extending through time. Children's usage differs from that of their elders. Moreover, Chaucer's usage differs from Shakespeare's and from ours. The sixth viewpoint is occupational. Each specialized job or hobby has its own ingroup vocabulary and phraseology. The seventh viewpoint is geographic. English usage extends throughout the world and has international, national, regional, and local dialects. All these viewpoints interact in creating the total situation of usage. One major function of dictionaries is to guide us to appropriate usage choices.

In this chapter we will consider dialects and dictionaries against the backdrop of the seven interlocking dimensions of modern English usage. Consistently, we will relate our information and insights to classroom teaching.

DIALECTS

Each person's uniqueness can be identified by an individual dialect or *idiolect*. No two people speak identically, even once. We can identify familiar voices on the telephone because of these tiny differences in speaking.

Idiolects are grouped into dialects, and every language is the sum of its dialects. All people use several dialects of their language, matching them rather skillfully to the many-faceted situations of everyday speech and writing.

A *dialect* is a distinct variety of a language used by a group of people who share interests, values, goals, and communication. Dialects differ from one another in pronunciation, grammar, and vocabulary. Speakers of a particular dialect form a *speech community*. Nearly every profession and hobby has its own specialized dialect—often labeled *jargon, cant,* or *argot*—which is not readily understood by those outside the group. Other speech communities are united by dialects reflecting their members' ethnic, national, or family backgrounds. We speak casually of "foreign accents" and "family sayings."

Dialects evolve because a spoken language changes constantly. We have noted that through time these changes accumulate. Geographical distance intensifies change. Even though two dialects may originate from the same language, if two groups of speakers transport the language to different locations, the dialects will diverge more and more from each other as well as from the mother tongue. This process explains how the mutually unintelligible Romance languages—French, Spanish, Portuguese, and Romanian, for example—all developed from the Latin of the ancient Roman Empire. Latin dialects of the soldiers and merchants who settled far away from Rome eventually developed into the Romance languages, so named because of their Roman source.

Many misinformed persons think that a dialect is "a corrupt or degenerate form of a language." Historically, this misconception reverses the facts. Dialects precede languages. For some cultural or economic reason, one of many dialects becomes the accepted standard for the country. In the fifteenth century, the dialect used in London became the beginning of "British Received Standard" because London was the center of commerce, politics, and culture. A similar development occurred in German. The Upper Saxon dialect in which Luther translated the Bible in the sixteenth century became the High German now taught in schools and used in important literary and cultural affairs in Germany, Austria, and Switzerland. Yet many other ancient folk dialects which date back to the Old High German of early medieval times still flourish.

In the United States no single regional dialect is the recognized national standard. Instead, each region has its own regional standard—the dialect of the educated people who live in that region. These regional dialects reflect our settlement and migration history.

On the eastern seaboard the dialects of New England and the Middle and Southern Atlantic states reflect the settlement patterns of the original thirteen colonies. Beginning their studies in the 1930s, linguistic geographers (called dialectologists) investigated this eastern area. On the basis of differences in pronunciation, vocabulary, and grammar, they identified three major dialect areas: Northern, Midland, and Southern. Later studies of regional American dialects have revealed that with the westward movement of the pioneers and later immigration, eastern dialects have blended and fused. The farther west one travels, the less clear and distinct the dialect boundaries become. Today differences are being further blurred due to television, radio, education, and the extreme mobility of the population.

Since the 1960s dialect study has increasingly focused on social dialects, paying attention to such influences as social class, economic level, race, racial isolation, occupation, group loyalties and values, mobility of population, and especially urbanization. Sociologists and linguists have pooled their resources in the new hybrid discipline called *sociolinguistics*. Using knowledge and techniques from both fields, sociolinguists have analyzed the dialects of urban centers like New York, Washington, D.C., Chicago, and Detroit and have discovered that the dialects of large cities are socially stratified. Certain speech markers identify socioeconomic classes and are recognized by all members of the speech community as social class markers.

For example, in New York City the absence of /r/ in phrases like *fourth floor* indicates social class. The better educated, younger, higher class speakers use /r/ more often than their less privileged and older fellow citizens. However, all New Yorkers "drop their r's" more or less; how often they do so signals their social class. All New Yorkers recognize the social signal of "r–dropping." They are quick to hear this and other sociolinguistic markers in the speech of other New Yorkers, even though they may be deaf to their own speech patterns.[1]

In recent years, sociolinguists have studied extensively

the nonstandard English dialect spoken in the urban ghettos of large cities throughout the United States. Since most people who speak this nonstandard dialect are black persons of low socioeconomic and educational status, it is often referred to as *black* English. These sociolinguistic dialect findings are important to teachers because children who speak this dialect regularly have the most severe problems adjusting to the middle-class attitudes and values of teachers, both black and white. History provides insight into these problems.

Whenever speakers of two mutually unintelligible languages are forced together in a situation where they must communicate, a *pidgin* language develops. A pidgin language uses the grammar and pronunciation patterns of one language and the vocabulary of the other to create a simplified system of communication. A pidgin passed on to the members of the next generation as their native language is called a *creole* language.

When the first English port was established on the West African Gold Coast about 1630, West African speakers of many mutually unintelligible but grammatically related African languages were forced together in slave camps. A pidgin English necessarily developed for communication between the traders and the Africans, as well as among the Africans themselves. This pidgin used African grammar and sounds but English vocabulary. In the English colonies in America, the descendants of these Africans spoke this pidgin as their mother tongue, and thus it became a creole language. The Gullah dialect still spoken in the isolated Carolina Sea Islands and the coastal regions of South Carolina, Georgia, and northeastern Florida still retains West African sound features and grammatical characteristics.

Throughout the years the West African creole has decreolized, that is, lost more and more of its typical creole features and thus has moved closer to standard English. Educated, middle-class black speakers use standard English, while male members of black adolescent and preadolescent urban street gangs speak a variety of black English with the fewest standard features. A spectrum of varieties lies in between. In defining this spectrum, some markers are more crucial than others. Teachers may wisely emphasize crucial markers if they can motivate their students to want to learn standard English. Here are five of the most crucial and consistent patterns.[2]

1. Lack of –s on third person singular present tense. This means that the speaker will say *he go* instead of *he goes*. West African languages have no verb inflections, so this marker is explainable in historical terms.

2. Multiple negation. This means more than one negative in a sentence with negative meaning: *didn't do nothin'* for *didn't do anything*. Double negation also occurs in other nonstandard dialects. But in West African languages every indefinite must be made negative to communicate negative meaning so that multiple negation like *never saw nobody nowhere nohow* is a regular feature of nonstandard black English. Certain negatives occur only in this dialect: *nobody didn't do it, didn't nobody do it, it wasn't no girls couldn't go with us.*

3. Zero possessive. This means the lack of the possessive suffix where standard English requires it: *my fahver frien'* for *my father's friend*, *man hat* for *man's hat*. West African languages also lack noun inflectional suffixes.

4. Invariant *be*. This means that *be* is used without a modal or inflection instead of the standard English *will be, would be, am, is,* or *are*. In addition, invariant *be* has a third possible meaning that does not occur in standard English at all: to express an habitual or customary action. Thus the sentence *He be busy* can mean:

   He will be busy or *He'll be busy*
   He would be busy or *He'd be busy*
   He is always busy.

5. Absence of forms of *be*. In other sentences *is* and *are* may be absent. (*Am* is usually present with the subject *I.*) This absence occurs when these forms are either main verbs or auxiliaries, as in the following examples.

   He a boy. That dude bad. We eatin' now.

Nonstandard black English differs systematically from other nonstandard dialects in more ways than just negation. For example, the nonstandard English dialect of the white Appalachian child has both *he's workin'* and *he's a–workin'*, while children who speak nonstandard black English use both *he workin'* and *he be workin'*. The first form in each nonstandard pair means that the person is doing a specific task nearby, while the second form in each pair means either that the person has a steady job or that he is away working somewhere. Thus both nonstandard dialects permit making a contrast that standard English cannot make as neatly.[3] The important fact is that these contrasts are patterned. They are not "sloppy English" or "careless speech," as linguistically uninformed persons often think.

Other significant differences can be explained by nonstandard phonological rules that correlate with standard grammatical inflections. These phonological facts may create homonyms in nonstandard black English that do not exist in standard English. Thus the nonstandard speaking child who is learning to read must recognize more homonyms than does the standard speaking child.

For example, in nonstandard black English the r is not pronounced before other consonants, at the ends of words, and often before a vowel. Thus the following pairs are homonyms:

> *guard* : *god*   *fort* : *fought*   *court* : *caught*

The same pattern is almost as frequent with *l*. "Dropping *l*'s" produces pairs of homonyms like the following:

> *toll* : *tow*   *help* : *hep*   *fault* : *fought*

In addition, some consonant clusters simplify at the ends of words. One consonant of several is absent, especially when the clusters end in /t/ or /d/ and /s/ or /z/ sounds. Thus the following pairs become homonyms:

> *past* : *pass*   *six* : *sick*   *hold* : *hole*

When several of these phonological facts combine, triple homoynms may result:

> *told* : *toll* : *toe*   *fort* : *fought* : *fault*

These phonological facts and others have important grammatical implications. For example, the absence of /r/ may make homonyms of the subject and possessive forms of *you* : *your*, and *they* : *their*. The absence of /l/ may make homonyms of personal pronouns and the forms used to express future time. The pairs *I* and *I'll*, *you* and *you'll*, *he* and *he'll*, *she* and *she'll*, *we* and *we'll*, and *they* and *they'll* may become homonyms. The absence of /t/ and /d/ affects the past forms of verbs that use these sounds for pronouncing the –*ed* inflection of the past tense and past participle. For example, *walk* and *walked* may become homonyms, as may *change* and *changed*. The absence of –*s* affects the third singular present tense of verbs and the plural and possessive of nouns. *Sing* and *sings* may fall together, as may *boy*, *boys*, and *boy's* and *boys'*.

In order to plan teaching strategies intelligently, teachers have a responsibility to try to understand their students' dialects. Otherwise teaching may do more harm than good. For example, when students consistently use no –*s* suffix in the third singular present tense and teachers constantly "correct" this usage, the students may overcorrect to produce:

I walks	we walks
you walks	you walks
he walks	they walks

Such overcorrection shows that the student has not understood the point. A wiser teaching strategy would be to focus the students' attention on the contrast between *he walks* (with –*s*) and every other form in the present tense (without –*s*). By practicing both forms, the students are more likely to understand the point of the lesson and not to overgeneralize the suffix.

Apparently, nonstandard speaking children can understand and read standard English better than they can speak or write it. Psycholinguistically oriented reading specialists stress the importance of understanding the difference between dialect interference and reading errors. Reading materials are normally written in standard English. If children read *he walks to school* as *he walk to school*, they are not making a reading mistake but are performing a remarkable linguistic translation from standard to nonstandard English. The translation reveals that they understand the underlying meaning of the sentence because they can express it in their own dialect. In other words, this is not a reading error but an example of dialect interference. Psycholinguistically oriented specialists hold that such "reading miscues" should not be penalized by the reading teacher because reading is essentially a process of understanding meaning not of merely pronouncing words.

Moreover, linguistically informed teachers separate the teaching of reading from the teaching of a new dialect. Once the student understands that words written on a piece of paper are meaningful whatever the dialect of the reader, the first major objective of education has been achieved. Later teaching can focus on learning to speak another dialect if the student wants to learn one.

For this basic reason, such special alphabets as the Initial Teaching Alphabet (ITA) are not a cure-all for reading problems. Instead of the twenty-six symbols of our traditional alphabet, ITA uses forty-four symbols. Thus it is often recommended as a more useful symbol system for teaching beginning reading. However, if nonstandard speaking children are forced to read the exact pronunciation of words in a dialect different from their own, they may become problem readers. Since the teacher's interpretation of the exact pronunciation of words will differ from their own, these children may think that the symbols are variable in pronunciation. A more effective plan would be to have the students read their own dialect from a page written in traditional orthography.

DICTIONARIES

Dr. Johnson originally intended his dictionary to "fix our language." However, when it was finally published in 1755 after nine years of work, he had learned that he could only "register the language," not "form it." In other words, he could neither keep the language from changing nor report all that people knew about their language.

In spite of this long-established fact, people in the United States tend to be "dictionary worshipers" rather than dictionary users. They consult a dictionary to find out "the correct meaning," as if there were only one dictionary and only one correct meaning. Neither assumption is true. There are many dictionaries and they differ from one another in many ways, as even a cursory examination of several will reveal. Furthermore, dictionaries describe usage; they do not prescribe single, simple, correct answers.

In the process of making a dictionary, lexicographers search for new words and new uses of old words. This information is discovered by collecting all kinds of written and recorded evidence. Each example is then listed on a separate citation slip along with its exact source, context, and date, and is filed. About ten million citation slips were gathered for the 450,000 words in *Webster's Third New International Dictionary of the English Language* published in 1961, twenty-seven years after its last previous edition, *Webster's New International Dictionary of the English Language*, second edition. *Webster's Third* has been updated several times since then as new citations have been collected.

Most dictionaries identify special dimensions of word usage by usage labels. These labels explain the situations in which the words have been used. Some characteristic labels are:

> *archaic* meaning "old, now used only in specialized contexts" (example: *thou*)
>
> *obsolete* meaning "no longer used" (example: *swoopstake*)
>
> *colloquial* meaning "characteristic of speech rather than writing"
>
> *formal, informal, slang* indicating the formality of the usage situation
>
> *dialectal, regional*, and names of specific geographic areas indicating place of usage
>
> *standard, nonstandard, substandard* indicating socioeconomic areas of usage.

The purpose of usage labels is to guide the dictionary user to appropriate choices. The exact meanings of usage labels vary from one dictionary to another. Each dictionary contains an explanatory section which gives the exact meaning of the labels it uses.

Children first use dictionaries to find out the semantic meanings and spellings of words. However, teachers mislead children if they automatically answer questions about spelling by saying, "Look it up in your dictionary." Unless the first three letters of an English word are known, it is difficult to locate in a dictionary. Making a child waste time searching blindly is poor teaching. Furthermore, not all dictionaries agree on the spellings of words or their exact uses. From the beginning the child should learn to use dictionaries as guides, not gods.

Teachers should broaden their students' use of dictionaries. For example, dictionaries provide semantic, grammatical, and etymological information. Part-of-speech labels explain the words' grammatical usages; and labels like *Latin*, *French*, or *German* document the historical derivation of words. As suggested in chapter 2, knowing the foreign source of a word may help students to understand its spelling. Superior classroom dictionaries also contain many special tables and indexes giving biographical, metrical, historical, or geographical information. Often dictionaries are a more conveniently available information source than are encyclopedias.

Because dictionaries are constantly useful in classrooms, they should be treated as tools for learning rather than as prescribers of usage laws. As we have seen, usage is a complex challenge, colored by many factors. No dictionary can ever record everything that can be known about the connotations of any word in all its possible contexts. In order for students to develop linguistic self-confidence, they should be encouraged to make intelligent guesses about meanings based on their previous experience with words in contexts.

SUGGESTIONS FOR STUDY AND DISCUSSION

1. How do the terms *slang, jargon, cant*, and *argot* differ in meaning? What characteristics do they have in common?

2. Investigate specific differences in pronunciation, grammar, and vocabulary among U.S. regional dialects. In this connection the following books are especially useful: *Discovering*

American Dialects by Roger W. Shuy, *The Story of American English* by J. N. Hook, and *English in Black and White* (especially chapter 2, "How Do Dialects Vary?") by Robbins Burling.

Listen to *Americans Speaking,* a dialect recording by John T. Muri and Raven I. McDavid, Jr., distributed by the National Council of Teachers of English. It contains samples of Northern, Midland, and Southern U.S. regional dialects. Another useful regional dialect recording is *Our Changing Language,* side 2, by Evelyn Gott Burack and Raven I. McDavid, Jr., also distributed by the National Council of Teachers of English.

3. Listen to Hal Holbrook's recordings *Mark Twain Tonight* (MD 43) and *Mark Twain Tonight–Volume II* (MD 44) (Listening Library of LP Recordings). Holbrook's rendition of Mississippi dialects as Mark Twain handled them is enlightening and enjoyable. This listening can be supplemented by reading *Down in the Holler: A Gallery of Ozark Folk Speech* by Vance Randolph and George P. Wilson.

4. Since motivation is an essential part of effective teaching, how can language arts teachers motivate students who speak nonstandard dialects to learn standard English? How important are age, parental influence, and home environment in motivation?

5. Listen to the recording *The Dialect of the Black American* (Western Electric Co., 1970). It briefly discusses some of the characteristics of black English and demonstrates that this dialect is a systematic means of communication. How convincing is the presentation? A variety of opinions can be expected in class discussion.

6. Belief in the "one-and-only-one correct answer myth" causes many people in the United States to feel "linguistic insecurity." In his study of New York City speech, the sociolinguist William Labov investigated his respondents' "index of linguistic insecurity." He had them listen to a recording of eighteen words, each pronounced in two different ways, numbered 1 and 2 on the answer sheet. They were asked to circle one number as the "correct" pronunciation and to check the number of the pronunciation they normally used.

The proportion of words with one pronunciation circled and the other checked was that person's index of linguistic insecurity. Try out the following list on a group of people in order to study the idea of linguistic insecurity. If you do not know two pronunciations for each word, check a large dictionary.

Joseph	1	2	length	1	2
catch	1	2	February	1	2
tomato	1	2	ketchup	1	2
diapers	1	2	escalator	1	2
aunt	1	2	new	1	2
often	1	2	tune	1	2
garage	1	2	avenue	1	2
humorous	1	2	because	1	2
vase	1	2	half	1	2

7. English is a world language. Familiarize yourself with a British point of view by reading *The Changing English Language* by Brian Foster and *The Use of English* by Randolph Quirk.

8. Investigate variant spellings in dictionaries by examining *Variant Spellings in Modern American Dictionaries* by Donald W. Emery and *A Comparative Study of Spellings in Four Major Collegiate Dictionaries* by Lee C. Deighton.

9. Examine some readers written in ITA and, if possible, discuss its use and value with several teachers who have used it in teaching beginning reading. What advantage does ITA have for teaching children to write?

NOTES

[1] William Labov, *The Social Stratification of English in New York City* (Arlington, Va.: Center for Applied Linguistics, 1966).

[2] Walt Wolfram, "Sociolinguistic Implications for Educational Sequencing," in *Teaching Standard English in the Inner City*, eds. Ralph W. Fasold and Roger W. Shuy (Arlington, Va.: Center for Applied Linguistics, 1970), p. 117.

[3] William A. Stewart, *Language and Communication Problems in Southern Appalachia* (Arlington, Va.: Center for Applied Linguistics, 1967), pp. 26–29. Reprinted in *Contemporary English: Change and Variation*, ed. David L. Shores.

PART TWO

APPLICATIONS OF LINGUISTICS TO LANGUAGE ARTS TEACHING

6

Applying Linguistics to Teaching Reading

OVERVIEW AND PURPOSE OF THE CHAPTER

Long before they read print, children read many other things. They read faces, television, and weather. That is, they mentally organize visual information and relate it to other parts of their knowledge. Reading print, however, is their most complex task. Some people never learn to read; many others learn only minimally and never become fluent readers. Even though vast resources of time and money are devoted to this educational problem, we still do not know how to teach everybody to read. Nevertheless, linguistics offers many helpful insights.

From studying language learning, linguistically trained teachers know that normal children enter school with a working knowledge of their native language. They have learned to speak and understand this language with little or no formal teaching, and they have done so at a very early age. Children learn their spoken language by making guesses and then testing these guesses on other people in their environment. In this process they notice differences, establish their own categories and rules, and learn through feedback whether their speech is making sense to other people. In school they must use these same cognitive skills in learning to read and write.

Structural linguists appeared as "reading specialists" in the 1960s when *Let's Read: A Linguistic Approach* was published. In this book Clarence A. Barnhart resurrected the theory formulated many years earlier by the great linguist, Leonard Bloomfield. This theory defined reading as a process of decoding letters, or graphemes, into sounds, or phonemes. Thus reading was presented as a process of translating visible information into audible information.

With some modifications this theory was extended by Charles C. Fries in *Linguistics and Reading*. In the first series of so-called "linguistic readers," Fries applied this theory to the teaching of reading. Soon other more or less similar series followed. Such series concentrated mainly on teaching words with fairly stable and predictable correspondences between letters and sounds. The books purposely omitted any meaningful illustrations that might help a reader guess at the pronunciation of a word. The reason was to eliminate all dependence on meaning and thus force children to rely entirely on phoneme–grapheme correspondences. Unfortunately, these structural ideas about teaching reading often are incorrectly labeled "the linguistic method."

In the 1970s the teaching of reading was enriched by new psycholinguistic insights. The term *psycholinguistic* is a blend of the words *psychological* and *linguistic*. Psychology and linguistics combined to produce a hybrid discipline, *psycholinguistics*, fusing relationships between the mind and the language. We will consider each half of the word *psycholinguistics*.

Two schools dominate the field of psychology today: behavioral and cognitive. Behavioral psychology teaches that learning is habit formation and that habits are formed by the reinforcement of a response to a stimulus. Behavioral psychology is relevent to habitual aspects of reading, like motivation. On the other hand, cognitive psychology teaches that learning is the acquisition of knowledge, not merely the formation of habits. The acquisition of knowledge cannot be perceived physically because it involves the perception and organization of information by the human brain. Cognitive psychology is relevant to deriving meaning from reading material.

The "linguistics" of *psychologuistics* is transformational-generative grammar, which agrees with cognitive psychology in its crucial concepts. The transformationalist believes that language has both a surface structure and a deep structure, and that there is no simple correspondence between the two. The more important structure is the deep structure, where meaning resides. Meaning cannot be perceived physically because it is abstract. In the deep structure of language, mere words are irrelevant. The surface structure furnishes audible sounds and visible letters to express that abstract deep meaning. Transformations are the bridge between deep and surface structures.

For example, we know that both sentences in the following pairs express essentially the same deep meaning even though their surface structures are different.

> Frank summed up the discussion.
> Frank summed the discussion up.
>
> Wasps are in this house.
> There are wasps in this house.
>
> Noah sang that song.
> That song was sung by Noah.

We also know that in the following sets of sentences, two sentences in each set are more like each other than either is like the third.

> David wanted Jerry to write.
> David asked Jerry to write.
> David promised Jerry to write.
>
> The student is hard to hear.
> The student is easy to hear.
> The student is eager to hear.

Therefore reading involves more than merely using your eyes to look and then making noises with your vocal organs. It also involves the brain. Efficient reading proceeds directly from written language to meaning without any mediation by oral reading. Only young children and their teachers and relatives read aloud frequently. Fluent readers choose to read silently because it is faster, and they can concentrate on the meaning. Never reading every word, fluent readers select the fewest and most informative cues to meaning and use them to guess what is not actually seen. The ability to make intelligent guesses about what has not yet been seen is as important in reading as the ability to guess what has not yet been heard is in listening. Both reading and listening are psycholinguistic guessing games.

In applying these psycholinguistic insights to the teaching of reading, Frank Smith denounces many traditional procedures. He admonishes teachers as follows.[1]

1. Do not teach any traditional "rules of reading." No rules of reading are simple and accurate enough to help anyone learn to read.

2. Do not teach phonics rules. Readers must grasp meaning before phonics rules can be applied. In other words, we do not know how to pronounce *read* until we grasp whether it is present /riyd/ or past /red/. Compare *He will read the book today* and *He read the book yesterday.* We do not know how to pronounce *present* until we know whether it is a noun /prezənt/ or a verb /priyzent/. Compare *My birthday presents are beautiful* and *My birthday presents problems.*

3. Always teach letters as parts of words, and words as parts of sentences. In the real world that is the way language works. The only realistic lists of words are ones like grocery lists or phone numbers and addresses. In each case the list has context. Yet would you entrust your grocery list to someone else—even a fluent reader—and expect to get what you wanted?

4. Accept sensible reading without worrying about word–perfect performance. Fluent readers read meanings, not words.

5. Encourage intelligent guessing. Reading quickly is easier than reading slowly. To read quickly, all readers make educated guesses.

6. Let readers make mistakes without penalty. We learn by our mistakes, and we need freedom to make them.

7. Let the context provide feedback to the reader. As teacher, hold back on your own feedback. Let readers help themselves to grow strong.

8. Do not worry about correcting eye movements. The problem is probably behind the eyeball anyway. Incorrect eye movements mean a reader is looking in the wrong place; they do not mean faulty vision. Knowing where to look involves the grasping of meaning, an activity of the brain, not of the eye. Drill in "correct eye movements" is a waste of time.

9. Wait a long time before labeling a student as "a problem reader." The teacher, the system, or the reading material may be the real problem.

10. Encourage self-confidence and enjoyment. Reading should bring its own reward. Reading is not learned competitively.

11. Forget spelling and other writing skills when teaching reading. Writing skills are irrelevant to learning to read. Reading may assist writing, but not vice versa.

12. Focus on the child, not on the method of teaching reading. With help and encouragement children will teach themselves to read.

The remainder of this chapter considers four linguistically based viewpoints from which a teacher can become aware of the patterns that surface in children's reading. Such awareness enables teachers to tap their own and their students' linguistic competence as native English speakers to aid in the process of learning to read. The first viewpoint involves relationships between dialects and reading. The second discusses the language–experience method of teaching beginning reading. The third is the "Cloze Procedure," a powerful and versatile tool for teaching and evaluating reading. The final viewpoint is the reading miscue analysis of Kenneth Goodman and his associates.

DIALECTS AND READING

The study of dialects suggests important psycholinguistic insights relevant to teaching reading. One is that no one speaks the standard written English used in reading textbooks. Everyone speaks a more natural, easy, conversational style: standard spoken colloquial or nonstandard spoken colloquial. These styles appear in reading materials only when conversation is directly quoted or imitated.

The following table gives examples of these three contrasting styles.[2]

Style 1: standard spoken colloquial
- a. We don't have any.
- b. There isn't anything you can do about it.
- c. He didn't have any that I wanted to look at.
- d. There's a box on the table.
- e. The kid got hit on the head.

Style 2: nonstandard spoken colloquial
- a. We don't have none.
- b. Ain't nothin' you can do about it.
- c. He didn't have none I wanted to look at.
- d. It's a box on the table.
- e. The kid got hit upside the head.

Style 3: standard written English
- a. We have none.
- b. Nothing can be done about it. / One can do nothing about it.
- c. He had none I cared to inspect.
- d. A box is on the table.
- e. The child was hit on the head.

Since reading texts are written in standard written English, children beginning to read must learn a new dialect, which they do not speak. Of course, styles 1 and 3 grade into each other; style 2 is more distinctively different from style 3. Therefore the task of the standard speakers is easier than that of their nonstandard-speaking peers.

However, the latter are able to understand standard English even though they do not speak it. They hear it on television, radio, and in contacts with standard speakers in their environment. In learning to read, they usually are able to grasp its underlying meaning. If asked to read aloud, however, they will naturally translate it into their nonstandard spoken colloquial. In teaching reading, psycholinguistically informed teachers accept nonstandard spoken colloquial just as they accept standard spoken colloquial. They recognize the effects of each child's dialect on the reading process. In other words, they concentrate on teaching reading and do not discourage children by constantly "correcting" their speech. Once children have learned to read, there is plenty of school time to teach them as much of styles 1 and 3 as they need.

Meanwhile teachers should treat all readers identically, whether they speak style 1 or style 2; that is, they should rephrase difficult passages into the spoken English children use. When style 1 children have trouble understanding a sentence, teachers automatically put it into other words. For example, teachers may rephrase a sentence like 3b: *One can do nothing about it* into 1b: *There isn't anything you can do about it*. However, teachers hesitate to rephrase it into 2b: *Ain't nothin' you can do about it*—even when they know the form. Reading teachers need to study dialects in order to help all children learn to read.

The next section of the chapter will be extremely helpful to speakers of nonstandard spoken colloquial and their teachers. It could even be the key to reading success.

THE LANGUAGE–EXPERIENCE METHOD

The language–experience method of teaching beginning reading gives new self-confidence to new readers, both young and old, by increasing their chances of success. In this method the children tape-record their own stories, which the teacher then writes or types on large sheets of paper for their future reading. In transcribing the stories, the teacher writes standard spellings to represent the vocabulary and grammar the student has dictated, and the teacher may also remove oral fillers. Then the student reads through the story with the teacher. Because the story is already known, the student's chances of success in reading are greatly enhanced.

The language–experience method works both for young children approaching reading for the first time and for children in upper grades who still do not read. The objective is the same with both types of readers: to help them learn to read. However, the process differs in distinctive ways.

Using the Method with Young Beginners

Suppose that a group of first graders had gone on a field trip to a nature center. There they saw many different birds, like parrots, cardinals, pheasants, woodpeckers, and eagles. They also saw many small wild animals, like raccoons, rabbits, squirrels, muskrats, and chipmunks. On their way back to school there was a thunderstorm, with lightning and heavy rain, but they were not frightened because they were having fun singing songs in the bus.

The normal follow-up on a field trip is that the children, as a group, compose a story about their adventures. The teacher writes the story on the board, and the children copy it as a writing exercise. Usually this story is short and simple so that the children can write it easily and quickly. Then their copies are displayed around the room or in the hall, but they are not used for a reading lesson. One way to introduce the language–experience method is to have the children use the written story for reading.

Teachers using the language–experience method encourage children to draw on the vocabulary and sentence structure of their oral style. Linguistically trained teachers know that the children's oral vocabulary is larger and more exact than their reading or writing vocabulary, and their oral sentence structure is much more complicated than the customary style of their reading texts. Children are capable of telling a much longer and more interesting story than they can write. Taping encourages freedom of expression. The teacher's transcription takes care of any spelling problems as in *raccoon* or *lightning*. In an ideal situation where a teacher has a small class and plenty of help, each child could tape the experience individually. These stories could then be bound into a book and used as a reader for the class.

Because the students have actually lived through the visit to the nature center, they know the meaning of the story before they start to read it. Since it is written in their own vocabulary, they know that no word is too difficult for them to read. Nevertheless, the teacher can help the students by asking before they start to read, "Are there any words you think you won't recognize in the story?" Some students might be unsure of words like *pheasant* or *thunder*. The teacher can then print such words with a felt-tip pen on word cards so that the unsure student can have them for reference. The student could be asked to find these words in the story. The main idea is for the teacher to do everything possible to insure the student's success in reading the story.

The creative teacher can find many uses for the language–experience method. For example, third graders could tape a humorous account of an experience and then read its written version to first graders. Sharing experiences is a powerful stimulus to learning. Or, second and third graders could make up a play in which several children participate. Later, as actors reading their parts, they can present the play to their classmates or to younger children.

Using the Method with Older Beginners

The language–experience method works for older beginners too—children in the upper grades who still do not read. Frequently these children have good minds and large, sophisticated oral vocabularies, but they will not read. Much attention has been given in the schools to providing "high interest–easy reading" for these students. The language–experience method focuses specifically on the student's personal interests, asking him or her to talk into a tape recorder about these interests and, after the teacher has transcribed them, to read about them.

Stories written by older beginners are more useful when read by their authors than by their classmates. A boy's account of repairing his cycle or a girl's about rigging a sailboat may contain too many technical words for their classmates who have other kinds of expertise.

The teacher or reading specialist can use various techniques to help the students prepare to read. The reading can be introduced by reminding the students that they dictated the reading material and therefore they already know what it says, and now they are going to read it. The teacher could add, "You remember what you said on the tape. Which words, if any, are you unsure about recognizing?" As the student identifies such words, the teacher can print them on word cards. The teacher can then ask, "Where do you find these words in the reading material?" The student can locate them by using the word cards for reference. Or, the teacher can ask the student to inspect the reading material before attempting to read it and thus spot any potential problem words, for which the teacher can make word cards. When the student feels confident to read, success is practically assured.

The language—experience method is a dynamic tool for drawing upon the students' oral skills in order to enhance learning to read. It is one of the best solutions to the problem of providing interesting, appropriate reading material for all children.

THE "CLOZE PROCEDURE"

Creating fluent readers is the true goal of reading instruction. Fluent readers are those who read easily and often both for pleasure and information. Reading teachers hope to guide students along the road to fluent reading as quickly and happily as possible. To this end, teachers provide a wealth of books and other reading materials of varied content and difficulty to stimulate children's interests and abilities. In order to do this effectively, teachers need a wide knowledge of books as well as a practical tool for matching books to children's reading comprehension. A book too difficult or too easy will not stimulate children to become fluent readers.

One effective tool is the "Cloze Procedure," an untimed reading test of a child's ability and a book's difficulty. It is inexpensive, easy to administer, versatile in use, and intimately correlated with the teacher's available reading materials. It is also firmly grounded in the psycholinguistic knowledge and intuitions of both teachers and students.

The term Cloze is related to the psychological concept of "closure," the tendency of the human mind to perceive things as whole and complete, even though they have gaps and missing elements. People consistently draw on their prior knowledge and experience to close the gaps and fill in the missing elements—in other words, to achieve closure.

Applied to reading, closure involves creating complete and meaningful sentences from incomplete sentences. Children can depend on only the surviving context and their own knowledge of grammar and semantics to reconstruct intelligently. For example, in the sentence *Fish swim and birds*_____, the grammatical and semantic relationships among the words cue the reader that *fly* is the omitted word. The "Cloze Procedure" applies this process to longer passages with many blank spaces.

When the "Cloze Procedure" is used to evaluate the difficulty of a book, a carefully selected passage of 250 or more words is used, with every fifth word omitted and replaced by a blank. The blanks are all the same size. To fill the gaps, the exact word used by the author must be supplied by the reader; synonyms are not acceptable. This condition is implicit in the fact that the author's style is the crucial variable.

When the "Cloze Procedure" is used for teaching, however, more or fewer words than one out of five may be omitted, depending on the teacher's instructional objectives and how difficult the children find the material. Then too, synonyms are acceptable and interesting to discuss with students. Synonyms reveal the extent of students' vocabulary as well as the depth, breadth, and quality of their understanding of the reading material. In addition, synonyms prove to students that there is a wide variety of grammatically and semantically appropriate answers within the context of a given passage.

For example, consider the following passage from *Charlotte's Web*,[3] as Wilbur, the pig, reflects upon his happy, secure life in the barn made possible by the sacrifice of Charlotte, the spider, his dear, dead friend.

Life in the barn ___1___ very good—night and ___2___, winter and summer, spring ___3___ fall, dull days and ___4___ days. It was the ___5___ place to be, thought ___6___, this warm delicious cellar, __7__ the garrulous geese, the __8__ seasons, the heat of __9__ sun, the passage of __10__, the nearness of rats, __11__ sameness of sheep, the __12__ of spiders, the smell __13__ manure, and the glory __14__ everything.

KEY

1. was	8. changing
2. day	9. the
3. and	10. swallows
4. bright	11. the
5. best	12. love
6. Wilbur	13. of
7. with	14. of

The linguistically oriented reading teacher will note that six of the fourteen omitted words are function words (and, with, the, the, of, of). Because function words are relatively few in number though high in frequency in the total language, the reader's choice is limited, and educated guessing is easier. Furthermore, the linking verb, was (blank 1) belongs to a relatively small class of verbs—linking verbs—limited essentially to was, appeared, seemed, became, or remained, and thus it, too, is easy to guess. In addition, the parallel syntax and the semantic content of winter and summer clearly cue the reader to the word day following night to fill blank 2. The choice Wilbur in blank 6 has no alternative; correctly filling this blank requires prior knowledge of the book Charlotte's Web. On the other hand, blanks 4 and 10 permit many alternate choices. Instead of the author's adjective bright, blank 4 could be sensibly filled by other adjectives such as:

sunny	gorgeous
sunshiny	vivid
wonderful	exciting
clear	interesting
happy	glorious

Blank 10 has several possible alternatives in addition to the author's noun *swallows:*

birds	larks
robins	butterflies
dragonfiles	(and so on)

Before children can perform a Cloze problem independently—for either evaluation or teaching—they will need careful explanations and group practice. Otherwise they may be frustrated by not understanding what is expected of them.

Comparisons of "Cloze Procedure" scores with scores on conventional comprehension tests reveal that a Cloze score of 44 percent is comparable to a conventional score of 75 percent. This correlation suggests that the reading material tested is suitable for use in a child's reading instruction with a teacher's help. A Cloze score of 57 percent is comparable to a conventional score of 90 percent. In such cases, the reading material is appropriate for the child's independent reading.[4]

Thus the "Cloze Procedure" is a valuable aid to teachers who are working to help children become fluent readers in the shortest, most direct ways possible. It truly opens wider the windows on the reading process.

MISCUE ANALYSIS

Miscue analysis is a clinical tool; in classroom use it can alert a teacher to the quality of a student's reading. This tool helps teachers comprehend reading as a psycholinguistic process of deriving meaning from groups of written symbols by means of graphic, phonological, grammatical, and semantic cues. *Graphic* cues are signals given by the letters, spelling, and punctuation of print, script, or other forms of writing. *Phonological* cues are signals given by the sounds, sound patterns, and intonation of the reading material. *Grammatical* cues are signals given by the sentence patterns, inflections, and function words of the reading material. *Semantic* cues are signals given by the reader's past experiences, as these relate to the concepts and vocabulary of the reading material. The graphic and phonological cues belong to the surface structure of the reading material. The grammatical and semantic cues belong to the underlying structure of the reading material.

A *miscue* is an observed response in oral reading that does not match the expected response. Kenneth Goodman says that a miscue is like "a window on the reading process." It permits a teacher to look into students' brains and discover what they are doing as they read. When children are comfortable in the situation and interested in the material, everything they do as readers is relevant to their purpose of getting meaning from the page. If teachers study their students' miscues psycholinguistically, they can learn how the children are using the cueing systems of the language.

For example, take the sentence,

> But I remember the cameras moving close to the crib and Mr. Baraby bending over and saying soothing things to Andrew—not too loudly.

One reader miscued on the beginning of the sentence, reading it

> But I remember that the camera moving

and then broke off to go back and correct the sentence to read

> But I remember the cameras moving close to the crib and Mr. Barny bending over saying some things to Andrew—but not too loud.

Thus this reader produced a sentence that is grammatically acceptable and semantically understandable even though *Baraby* became *Barny*, the *and* after *over* was omitted, *soothing* became *some*, *but* was added before *not*, and *loudly* was read as *loud*. The reader demonstrated competence in using the grammatical and semantic cueing systems of the language to get meaning from reading.

On the other hand, the student who reads

> Her wings were floated quickly at her sides

instead of the printed sentence

> *Her wings were folded quietly at her sides*

is being fooled by the graphic similarities between *floated/folded* and *quickly/quietly,* and is failing to use the grammatical or semantic cues to get meaning in reading. As readers become more proficient, they pay less and less attention to graphic cues and more and more to grammatical and semantic cues.

Readers test their predictions by noting whether their reading sounds sensible. By doing so, they are using their language competence to achieve meaning. The more real–world experience they bring to the reading, the more successful they are. The richer the students' conceptual world, the easier it is for them to read. Nonstandard speakers make different judgments on the cue systems because their spoken dialect differs from standard spoken English. The linguistically oriented teacher will recognize that the child who reads the sentence

> *I asked Tom if he wanted to go to the picture that was playing at the Howard*

as

> *I asks Tom do he want to go to the picture that be playing at the Howard*

is performing a double intellectual feat by getting the meaning of the sentence in standard English and then translating that meaning into the equivalent sentence pattern in black English. These miscues are explainable as dialect interferences.

The most important criterion of readers' efficiency is whether their reading makes sense. Good readers tend to correct only those miscues that result in a loss of meaning, not even noticing a miscue that does not alter meaning significantly. On the other hand, poor readers are conscious of their oral performance but ignorant of what they have read.

A linguistically informed teacher can incorporate insights from miscue analysis in teaching reading. By understanding and emphasizing process, language, and meaning in teaching reading, the teacher is helping children enhance their own linguistic competence.

SUGGESTIONS FOR STUDY AND DISCUSSION

1. The following reading selection, "The Wonder of the Monarchs," is from Bill Martin's *Sounds of Laughter* (New York: Holt, Rinehart and Winston, 1966, pp. 192–197). This book is one of the *Sounds of Language Readers*, an excellent reading series, thoroughly grounded in psycholinguistic insights about the reading process and the nature of children and language. Martin's selection is adapted from Harvey Gunderson's more difficult Young Owl Book, *The Wonder of the Monarchs* (New York: Holt, Rinehart and Winston, 1964).

In the following "Cloze Procedure" sample, every fifth word is omitted and replaced by blanks that are all the same size. Fill in the blanks without consulting the key. Take as much time as you need in order to use all the available cues; the test is untimed. Now many words did you miss? For how many words did you supply adequate synonyms? Now administer the untimed test to a group of students. When you type it for students' use, do not number the blanks or give the key, since the children are to fill in the blanks without help.

As previously explained, the procedure can be used either for evaluation of the difficulty of a selection or for the teaching of reading.

When the procedure is used for evaluation, no synonyms are acceptable. The exact words of the selection are one aspect of its ease or difficulty. Therefore the only correct answers are the words in the key, the actual words of the selection. In the light of your findings, how many of the students achieved a score of 44 percent and could therefore use this selection for reading instruction with a teacher's help? How many students achieved a score of 57 percent and could therefore use this selection for independent reading?

When the procedure is used for teaching reading, synonyms are acceptable. Where does each child supply appropriate synonyms? Do these synonyms differ from your own? In what ways? Which cueing systems does the student use well? Poorly? Explain your decisions.

The Monarch caterpillar is ___1___ from a tiny egg. ___2___ caterpillar is only one ___3___ of an inch long ___4___ it is newly hatched, ___5___ it grows quickly. In ___6___ days it is about ___7___ half-inch long. In two ___8___ it is fullgrown.

A ___9___ sheds its skin four ___10___ during its growing period. ___11___ the two-week growing period ___12___ gains 3,000 times its ___13___ weight and nearly 30 ___14___ its original length.

Then ___15___ caterpillar attaches itself to ___16___ twig to begin a ___17___ change. It wriggles out ___18___ its old skin and ___19___ body becomes a bright ___20___. This creature is no ___21___ a caterpillar, but a ___22___. Within the glossy green ___23___ the outline of a ___24___ body begins to appear.

___25___ about eight days the ___26___ changes color, from green ___27___ orange and black. The ___28___ of the Monarch butterfly's ___29___ are beginning to show ___30___. All organs of the ___31___ body have disappeared by ___32___, and organs useful to ___33___ butterfly have formed.

___34___ last it is the right ___35___! The transparent chrysalis cracks ___36___, and the Monarch butterfly ___37___ out, head first.

The ___38___ wings are very small ___39___ its abdomen is very ___40___. This is so because ___41___ abdomen is filled with ___42___ fluid that must be ___43___ into the wings. As ___44___ wings become inflated, the ___45___ gets smaller.

It takes ___46___ hours for the wings ___47___ dry, and another four ___48___ five hours for them ___49___ become strong.

From egg, ___50___ caterpillar, to chrysalis, to butterfly— three or four generations of Monarchs complete this cycle in a single summer.

KEY

1. born	26. chrysalis
2. The	27. to
3. tenth	28. colors
4. when	29. wings
5. but	30. through
6. three	31. caterpillar's
7. a	32. now
8. weeks	33. the
9. caterpillar	34. At
10. times	35. moment
11. During	36. open
12. it	37. crawls
13. original	38. butterfly's
14. times	39. and
15. the	40. large
16. a	41. the
17. miraculous	42. a
18. of	43. pumped
19. its	44. the
20. green	45. abdomen
21. longer	46. several
22. chrysalis	47. to
23. chrysalis	48. or
24. butterfly's	49. to
25. In	50. to

2. To improve your understanding of miscue analysis, tape-record a child's oral reading of a passage not previously read and difficult enough to cause reading miscues. Do not prompt or interrupt the child during the reading. Record about forty miscues and analyze the last twenty-five. List them in two parallel columns, one labeled "Text" and the other labeled "Reader." In addition, number the sentences in the text and, in two other parallel columns, record the number of each sentence and the number of miscues each contains. Then analyze your recording by using the following "Reading Miscue Inventory—Short Form." It is part of a kit, *Reading Miscue Inventory*, compiled by Yetta Goodman and Carolyn

Burke.[5] The complete kit consists of a manual, coding sheets, profile sheets, selections for reading, cassette tapes of children reading, typescripts for marking miscues, and precoded work sheets and profile sheets to accompany the cassettes. These materials are more useful to reading specialists and diagnosticians than to reading teachers. However, teachers can use the short form to improve their understanding of the psycholinguistic cueing systems involved in the reading process.

READING MISCUE INVENTORY—SHORT FORM[6]

Words in Context

Questions a, b, and c are to be answered for each substitution miscue. Under the column headed "Text" list each item that is involved in a substitution miscue. Next to it, under the column heading "Reader," list the item which the reader substituted. Answer the following questions for each pair of items.

    a. Graphic similarity: How much do the two words *look* alike?

    b. Sound similarity: How much do the two words *sound* alike?

    c. Grammatical function: Is the grammatical function of the reader's word the same as the grammatical function of the text word? (To help answer this question, read the text sentence with the reader's miscue in it.)

Structure and Meaning

Questions d, e, f, and g are to be answered for each sentence containing miscues. Number each sentence in the text, and place the numbers for sentences containing miscues under the column headed "Sentence Number." Next to this, in the column headed "Number of Miscues," indicate the number of miscues contained in each sentence.

    d. Syntactic acceptability: Is the sentence involving the miscues syntactically (grammatically) acceptable?

    e. Semantic acceptability: Is the sentence involving the miscues semantically (meaningfully) acceptable?

    f. Meaning change: Is there a change in meaning involved in the sentence?

    g. Correction and semantic acceptability: Do corrections by the reader make the sentence semantically acceptable?

3. One linguistically based suggestion for minimizing dialect interference in teaching reading to children who speak non-standard black English is to use reading materials written in their mother tongue. Such materials retain the grammar of the child's dialect but are transcribed into standard spelling. In this way the children do not face the double problem of learning to read while simultaneously learning a new spoken dialect.

Two alternatives are proposed for the preparation of such reading materials. First, teachers may transcribe the children's own dictation on language–experience charts to be read back by the children. This alternative enables the children to understand the process of changing spoken sounds into written words and then reconverting them into speech sounds. The second alternative is "dialect readers." These contain reading materials translated into nonstandard grammar but written in standard spelling. Read the following passage from the Bible, which is an example of this type of material. What advantages and/or disadvantages do you foresee in using material like this in the classroom?

John 3:1–17

It was a man named Nicodemus. He was a leader of the Jews. This man, he come to Jesus in the night and say, "Rabbi, we know you a teacher that come from God, cause can't nobody do the things you be doing 'cept he got God with him."

Jesus, he tell him say, "This ain't no jive, if a man ain't born over again, ain't no way he gonna get to know God."

Then Nicodemus, he ask him, "How a man gonna be born when he already old? Can't nobody go back inside his mother and get born."

So Jesus tell him, say, "This ain't no jive, this the truth. The onliest way a man gonna get to know God, he got to get born regular and he got to get born from the Holy Spirit. The body can only make a body get born, but the Spirit, he make a man so he can know God. Don't be surprised just cause I tell you that you got to get born over again. The wind blow where it want to blow and you can't hardly tell where it's coming from and where it's going to. That's how it go when somebody get born over again by the Spirit."

So Nicodemus say, "How you know that?"

Jesus say, "You call yourself a teacher that teach Israel and you don't know these kind of things? I'm gonna tell you, we talking about something we know about cause we already seen it. We telling it like it is and you-all think we jiving. If I tell you about things you can see and you-all think we jiving and don't believe me, what's gonna happen when I tell about things you can't see? Ain't nobody gone up to Heaven 'cept Jesus, who come down from Heaven. Just like Moses done hung up the snake in the wilderness, Jesus got to be hung up. So that the peoples that believe in him, he can give them real life that ain't never gonna end. God really did love everybody in the world. In fact, he loved the people so much that he done gave up the onliest Son he had. Any man that believe in him, he gonna have a life that ain't never gonna end. He ain't never gonna die. God, he didn't send his Son to the world to act like a judge, but he sent him to rescue the peoples in the world."[7]

4. In order to understand how difficult it is to read a word list, make two lists—one a completely random list of words, the other a grocery list. Ask a classmate to do the same and exchange lists. Which list is faster to read? After reading the lists, how many words can you recall from each list? Which list would you rather be asked to memorize? Which list would make more sense as a spelling list? Discuss what problems each of you would have in bringing home exactly what is written on the grocery lists.

5. Use the textbook evaluation form in the appendix to analyze, study, and evaluate one or more of the teacher's editions of the readers in Bill Martin, Jr.'s series *Sounds of Language.* How does Martin capitalize on the language–experience method of teaching reading?

NOTES

[1] "Twelve Easy Ways to Make Learning to Read Difficult and One Difficult Way to Make It Easy," in *Psycholinguistics and Reading* (New York: Holt, Rinehart and Winston, 1973), pp. 183–196.

[2] Robbins Burling, *English in Black and White* (New York: Holt, Rinehart and Winston, 1973), p. 150.

[3] E. B. White (New York: Harper and Row, 1952), p. 183.

[4] John R. Bormuth, "The Cloze Readability Procedure," *Elementary English*, 45 (1968), 433.

[5] (New York: Macmillan, 1972).

[6] Adapted from Carolyn Burke, "Preparing Elementary Teachers to Teach Reading," in *Miscue Analysis: Applications to Reading Instruction*, Kenneth S. Goodman, ed., (Urbana, Ill.: Educational Resources Information Center/Clearinghouse on Reading and Communication Skills/National Council of Teachers of English, 1973), p. 23.

[7] Walter A. Wolfram and Ralph W. Fasold, "Toward Reading Materials for Speakers of Black English: Three Linguistically Appropriate Passages," in *Teaching Black Children to Read*, eds. Joan C. Baratz and Roger W. Shuy (Arlington, Va.: Center for Applied Linguistics, 1969), pp. 150–151.

7

Applying Linguistics to Teaching Literature

OVERVIEW AND PURPOSE OF THE CHAPTER

Throughout the time that children are learning to become fluent readers, their teachers are striving to create lovers of literature. The teaching of reading and the teaching of literature proceed simultaneously, with each reinforcing the other. Linguistic insights and knowledge are equally relevant to teaching reading and literature.

In the education of language arts teachers, reading and literature are usually separated even though literature unifies all the activities of the elementary language arts curriculum. Robert Hogan, long-time executive secretary of the National Council of Teachers of English, says that reading, composition, and language are inextricably bound together and that the study of literature pervades all three.

In teaching literature, language arts teachers regularly use questions to help students comprehend the material they have read. Ordinarily these questions pay little or no attention to the literature's language. Knowledge of linguistics can supplement other teaching strategies by focusing on the language of the literature and showing how it contributes to the reader's total literary experience. A set of twenty linguistic questions has been developed to help teachers use linguistic knowledge and insights to improve their teaching of literature.

The next part of this chapter lists and explains these questions and then relates them to the linguistic information presented in the first part of this book. This section can become a reference guide for teachers as they apply the linguistic questions in teaching literature.

The chapter continues with separate discussions of five literary selections—called "lit bits" for short—arranged in an order of increasing difficulty. Each discussion is divided into four parts:

1. linguistic teaching goals,
2. linguistic analysis,
3. teaching plan,
4. follow-up evaluation activities.

In the five linguistic analyses, the application of each linguistic question is illustrated at least once so that the teacher has an example for reference. A few of the questions are applied to each lit bit. The five teaching plans show how teachers can adapt the linguistic questions for use with their students. Remember—*the linguistic questions are for teachers to use, not students.*

LINGUISTIC QUESTIONS WITH EXPLANATIONS

1. What are the unusual words and what do they mean in this context? What other meanings for them do you know? What synonyms could be substituted for them in this context?

As explained in the discussion of dictionaries in chapter 5, words frequently have more than one meaning. Sometimes children know one meaning for a word, but the meaning is not proper for the context in which the word appears. Locating and explaining problem words is the teacher's first task in helping students understand literature.

2. What part of speech is this word in this context? What other part(s) of speech can it be in other contexts?

A word's part of speech, as defined in chapter 3, depends on its use in a sentence. Many words can be more than one part of speech. *Round* is an example.

as a noun: Gary played a *round* of golf.
as a verb: Did the car *round* the corner on two wheels?
as an adjective: Joel bought a *round* box.
as an adverb: The wheel turns *round*.
as a preposition: We run *round* the playground.

If children misjudge a word's part of speech, they may have problems comprehending the literature being read.

3. What is the proportion of long to short words? How does it affect the difficulty of the selection?

To find the long words, pronounce them aloud and count the number of syllables. Do not be fooled by the spelling. From the discussion of relationships between sounds and spelling in chapter 2, we know that spelling is often a false guide to pronunciation. Thus the four-letter word *baby* has two syllables but the seven-letter word *through* has only one. If many words in a lit bit have three or more syllables, children may fear that the selection is difficult to read and understand.

4. What is the author's policy about repeating words as contrasted with using a variety of synonyms? What are the advantages and/or disadvantages of repetition?

As suggested in chapter 5, the study of dictionaries alerts teachers and students to the existence of synonyms. However, authors may deliberately repeat a word instead of using a synonym. The repetition may be to emphasize the word, to play on its sound, or for other reasons. Accidental, meaningless repetition is rare in good literature.

5. If the author uses intensifiers, how does this use strengthen or weaken the selection?

As explained in the discussion of adjectives and adverbs in chapter 3, intensifiers are a special group of adverbs that modify adjectives and adverbs but not verbs. *Very* is the most common intensifier and may be used for emphasis, but if overused, it can lose its force. In analyzing an author's use of intensifiers, we guess the reasons for using them and judge the value of those reasons.

6. Which words cluster into collocations to emphasize various ideas in the selection?

Collocations are groups of related words that occur close together in a literary selection. The words may be related by derivational affixes into word families, as discussed in "How Sounds Contribute to Meaning" in chapter 2. In addition, words may be related by meaning, as explained in the discussion of dictionaries in chapter 5. For example, a group of words clustering into a collocation about the idea of springtime might include *April, bloom, bud, flower, fresh, grass, green, grow, mud, shower, sunshine, warm, wet,* and many others.

7. What is the proportion of factual to evaluative adjectives? How does it affect the tone of the selection?

Applying the information on adjectives given in chapter 3, teachers may identify two types that contrast in meaning and effect: *factual* and *evaluative*. Factual adjectives refer to facts that can be perceived by the five senses—*green, cold, wet*— whereas evaluative adjectives express an opinion or value judgment—*good, lovely, wonderful.* Some adjectives cannot be clearly and easily classified into either category; these words provide interesting class discussions. Authors' adjectives can give a distinctively factual or evaluative tone to their writing. When discussing the tone, center on whether it is appropriate to the author's purposes as you and the students interpret them. Teachers should expect and accept more than one opinion.

8. What comparisons are used? Are any of them clichés? How do the comparisons strengthen or weaken the literary selection?

Chapter 3 explained that comparisons are one type of adverbialization. The children can note now that if comparisons are too worn-out to carry fresh meaning, they are called *clichés.* However, an adult's cliché may seem fresh and vivid to a child to whom it is new. Therefore, when teachers are linguistically aware of children's processes of language acquisition, they encourage discussion of the accuracy of the comparison rather than its novelty.

9. **How frequently are regional and/or social dialect markers used? What reasons might the author have for using dialects and how valid are these reasons?**

Here teachers can utilize their linguistic knowledge of dialects (chapter 5). Authors often bring characters to life by having them use dialectal words, structures, and pronunciations. If the markers enhance the characterizations, they serve a valid artistic purpose. However, dialect can easily be overdone, making the selection difficult to read and understand.

10. **What complications are caused by the historical development of our language?**

The history of English was discussed in chapter 4. In reading literature, children may be puzzled by old-fashioned words and meanings. Teachers might be surprised when children are mystified by words that are only a few years old from the teacher's adult viewpoint. The linguistically informed teacher anticipates and clarifies such mysteries.

11. **How frequent is the definite article** the **as opposed to the indefinite article** a (an)? **How does the frequency reflect the author's relationship to the reader?**

In the discussion of noun phrases in chapter 3, we learned that the definite article the and the indefinite article a (or an before vowels) are determiners, which indicate that a noun is coming up in the sentence. The frequent use of definite the seems to imply that the author is close to the reader and is saying, "You know what I mean. We understand each other." For example, the many uses of the in "The Star-Spangled Banner" suggest that the author and the reader are united in their knowledge and feelings about "the land of the free and the home of the brave." If such intimacy is intended, the use of the is effective; otherwise it is not. The readers decide.

12. **What is the distribution of sentence types: fragments, basic sentences, sentences with joining transforms, inserting transforms, or both? How does this distribution affect the reading ease or difficulty of the selection?**

With chapter 3 as reference guide, teachers can analyze any literary selection to determine its grammatical complexity. This analysis can help them judge if it is appropriate for their students. Although school-age children use all types of transformations in their speech, an overly complex sentence structure may cause problems in reading and comprehension. When in doubt, teachers should choose a simpler selection or be ready to paraphrase the difficult grammar for their students.

13. How frequently are imperatives, with and without *you,* **used? What reasons might explain their use in this context?**

Since the imperative always occurs with *you* expressed or understood (as explained in chapter 3), the author using imperatives is speaking directly to the reader. This fact adds a face-to-face intimacy to the writing, which the reader may feel without understanding the feeling. Focusing on the imperatives could supply an explanation.

14. If the word order is inverted, how can it be rearranged into normal, Modern English? What reasons might explain its inversion and how valid are these reasons?

The analysis of basic sentences in chapter 3 showed that the normal order of words in English sentences is subject–verb–object. Any other order easily confuses students. Therefore teachers need to untangle and explain inversions, which are sometimes used by prose writers for emphasis or by poets for rhyme. As explained in discussing the history of our language, earlier English permitted more flexible word order in sentences because many inflectional suffixes signaled how words were related to one another. In Modern English word order is crucial because most inflectional sufflixes have been lost. Therefore, teachers need to give students more help on older literature—particularly poetry—where unexpected word order is especially frequent.

15. How could a change in intonation change the meaning of a particular word or sentence in the selection?

In "How Sounds Contribute to Meaning" (chapter 2), *intonation* is defined as "the rhythm and music of speech." Stress, pitch, and pause are three intonation signals of meaning. In actual speech we can pronounce any sentence in many different ways. Each change affects meaning. Children can explore different possibilities, experimenting freely with various intonation changes as they read literature aloud.

16. How powerfully do verbs carry meaning without adjectives or manner adverbs to help them?

Chapter 3 explained that linking verbs may be followed by adjectives and that any sentence may end with an adverb. However, many authors tend to use verbs that clearly include the adjective or adverb meaning. In other words, these authors would use *obey* instead of *be obedient, apologize* instead of *be apologetic, doubt* instead of *be doubtful, run* instead of *go swiftly, yell* instead of *speak loudly, grip* instead of *hold firmly.* Recognizing powerful verbs increases students' understanding of literature and may encourage them to follow the same pattern in their own writing.

17. What peculiarities in spelling or punctuation are present? How can they be explained?

Unusual spellings may be archaic as in the King James Bible, or regionally dialectal as in *The Jack Tales,* or both regionally and socially dialectal as in Joel Chandler Harris's Uncle Remus stories. Unusual punctuation may be old-fashioned as in Grimm's Fairy Tales or whimsically individualistic as in the poetry of E. E. Cummings. Generally, unusual spelling or punctuation should be explained to students, or at least called to their attention.

18. How does the author use sounds in the literary selection?

Without using technical terms like *rhyme* or *onomatopoeia,* teachers can explain that sounds may reflect many meanings to the reader. The meanings may be pleasant or unpleasant, depending on the author's purposes and skill. Discussing the effects of sounds deepens students' understanding of literature.

19. How does the author use rhythm in the literary selection?

Children normally have a well-developed sense of rhythm and can easily appreciate the rhythms of literature. They can beat out the rhythms of poetry and rhythmic prose with their hands or move to its beat with their whole bodies. Understanding the author's use of rhythm intensifies their involvement with literature.

20. In analyzing a poem, what tension, if any, can be found between the rhythms of natural speech and the metrical patterns of the poem?

As we know from chapter 2, English speech has certain regular intonation patterns. Classical metrical patterns do not always match these patterns. Discussing the mismatch helps students understand that skillful poetry readers balance the two—emphasizing normal speech rhythm sufficiently to avoid a singsong, while emphasizing the meter enough to maintain a poetic effect.

LIT BITS

From *Millions of Cats* by Wanda Gág[1]

Once upon a time there was a very old man and a very old woman. They lived in a nice clean house which had flowers all around it, except where the door was. But they couldn't be happy because they were so very lonely.

"If we only had a cat!" sighed the very old woman.

"A cat?" asked the very old man.

"Yes, a sweet little fluffy cat," said the very old woman.

"I will get you a cat, my dear," said the very old man.

And he set out over the hills to look for one. He climbed over the sunny hills. He trudged through the cool valleys. He walked a long, long time and at last he came to a hill which was quite covered with cats.

> Cats here, cats there,
> Cats and kittens everywhere,
> Hundreds of cats,
> Thousands of cats,
> Millions and billions and trillions of cats.

Millions of Cats is a picture book, which could be read to children even before they are ready to read it themselves. This selection begins the story about how a lonely old man and woman found their very own cat. *Millions of Cats* is suitable reading for primary school children, six and seven years old.

Linguistic Teaching Goals. In teaching this lit bit, the teacher might have two linguistic goals. The first might be to help students recognize that a variety of rhythm and sound effects enhances the effectiveness of literature. The second goal might be to help students understand that words are often repeated to achieve definite purposes of the author, probably most often for emphasis of key ideas and characters.

Linguistic Analysis. The following linguistic questions focus the teacher's linguistic analysis.

4. What is the author's policy about repeating words as contrasted with using a variety of synonyms?
5. If the author uses intensifiers, how does this use strengthen or weaken the selection?
18. How does the author use sounds in the literary selection?
19. How does the author use rhythm in the literary selection?
20. In analyzing a poem, what tension, if any, can be found between the rhythms of natural speech and the metrical patterns of the poem?

Using linguistic questions 4 and 5 together, the teacher notes that the following words are repeated as indicated.

very	7 uses	*and*	6 uses
cats	11 uses	*woman*	3 uses
old	6 uses	*man*	3 uses

Often words are repeated because they are important in the context, as *cats, old, man,* and *woman* are in this lit bit. In addition, the intensifier *very* increases the importance of the words it modifies. In this lit bit these words are *old* and *lonely.* Furthermore, the conjunction *and* is a signal of joining transformation. Its use here ties together *the very old man* and *the very old woman,* just as the *ands* in the last line tie together the *millions* and *billions* and *trillions of cats.*

Using linguistic questions 18, 19, and 20 together, the teacher observes that, although the lit bit is not a poem, it has a poetical effect, mainly because of its refrain:

> Cats here, cats there,
> Cats and kittens everywhere,
> Hundreds of cats,
> Thousands of cats,
> Millions and billions and trillions of cats.

This poetical effect is intensified by the frequent repetition of the sounds /k/ and /s/, and by the internal rhyme in the last line: *millions—billions—trillions*.

Teaching Plan. First read aloud the whole story of *Millions of Cats* with the children. The refrain appears seven times, in whole or in part. The children soon learn to listen for it, to chant it aloud with the teacher, and to move with its rhythm. Ask the children, "Why do you say that part with me? How does it make you feel? What sounds do you hear often in that part?" (A great variety of answers can be expected.)

Then, extending the focus to include other forms of repetition, ask, "What word is in the story the most often?" (*Cats.*) "Count how many times. Why do you think this word is used so many times?" (Because the story is about cats.) "What other word also means cats?" (*Kittens.*) "What is the difference between cats and kittens?" (Kittens are young cats.) "Who else besides cats and kittens is important in the story?" (The *very old man* and the *very old woman.*) "Count how many times each of these names is used in the story. Notice that *very* appears seven times. Can you find all seven of them? If we left out all the *very*s, how would that change the meanings of *so very lonely, the very old man*, and *the very old woman?*" (It would make them less lonely and less old.) "Then why do you think the writer of the story put in *very?*" (To tell us that the man and woman were really lonelier than lonely and older than old.) "How does that make you feel?" (We feel very sorry for the very old man and the very old woman because they are so very lonely. This feeling helps us understand why the refrain about the millions and billions and trillions of cats makes us feel happy.)

If the children are still interested in the idea of repetition, point out that *and* appears six times and ask what the meaning of *and* is. (It is like the plus sign in math. It joins things together.) What words does it join in the story? (*A very old man* and *a very old woman, millions* and *billions* and *trillions of cats.*) The children can practice joining words together. (Examples: *Billy and Herbert; boy and girl; laugh and play; bright and happy; peanut butter and jelly.*)

Now, as a final step, reread with the children the entire story of *Millions of Cats* to see if it has become more meaningful because of the lesson.

Follow-up Evaluation Activities.

1. Ask the children to think about games which use refrains that make them feel like moving, marching, or dancing. Examples are "London Bridge Is Falling Down" and "The Farmer in the Dell." Let the children play the games.
2. Children can experiment with the intensifier *very* in telling or writing stories, using it to make meanings stronger.
3. Children can experiment with using *and* instead of the plus sign in addition problems. They can decide how *and* is different from the plus sign. Have them discuss which is better and why.

From *Once a Mouse* by Marcia Brown[2]

Fortunately, the hermit was nearby, and with a gesture, he changed the dog into a handsome, royal tiger. Now, imagine the pride of that tiger! All day long he peacocked about the forest, lording it over the other animals. The hermit missed nothing of all this, and chided the beast. "Without me," he would say to him, "you would be a wretched little mouse, that is, if you were still alive. There is no need to give yourself such airs." The tiger felt offended and humiliated. He forgot all the good he had received from the old man.

"No one shall tell me that I was once a mouse. I will kill him!"

But the hermit read the tiger's mind.

"You are ungrateful! Go back to the forest and be a mouse again!"

So the proud and handsome tiger turned back into a frightened, humble, little mouse, that ran off into the forest and was never seen again. And the hermit sat thinking about big—and little . . .

This lit bit ends *Once a Mouse*, a folktale from India about a hermit who rescues a mouse from a series of progressively more powerful animals who attack him. Finally a tiger threatens the mouse, who then has the form of a dog. *Once a Mouse* is suitable reading for middle elementary school children, ages seven to nine.

Linguistic Teaching Goals. In teaching this lit bit, the teacher might have four linguistic goals. The first might be to help students realize that it is interesting to discuss words and that such discussion often helps us understand literature more fully. A second linguistic goal might be to have students observe some concrete examples of grammatical concepts in the specific, clear contexts of the story. A third linguistic goal might be to show students that language changes through time. A fourth linguistic goal might be to explain to the students how grammatical structure and semantic meaning are related to punctuation.

Linguistic Analysis. The following linguistic questions focus the teacher's linguistic analysis.

1. **What are the unusual words and what do they mean in this context? What other meanings for them do you know? What synonyms could be substituted for them in this context?**
2. **What part of speech is this word in this context? What other part(s) of speech can it be in other contexts?**
3. **What is the proportion of long to short words? How does it affect the difficulty of the selection?**
6. **Which words cluster into collocations to emphasize various ideas in the selection?**
10. **What complications are caused by the historical development of our language?**
13. **How frequently are imperatives, with or without *you*, expressed? What reasons might explain their use in this context?**
17. **What peculiarities in spelling or punctuation are present? How can they be explained?**

Combining linguistic questions 1, 2, and 10, the teacher can consider three interesting words: *peacocked, lording,* and *hermit.* Although *peacock* is usually a noun—the name of a large bird—here the *-ed* suffix signals that is being used as a verb, meaning "to behave like a peacock." In the same way, the *-ing* suffix on *lording* signals that *lord* is being used here as a verb meaning "to behave like a lord," although it too is usually a noun—the name of a member of the aristocracy in countries that have such a social class. The third interesting word, *hermit,* today means "a recluse or monk." Here, as in other folktales, it means "a man who can work magic," like changing mice into tigers. The historical dimension of our language is involved.

Using linguistic question 3, the teacher discovers five words with three to six syllables.

> *3–6 syllables*
> fortunately
> imagine
> offended
> humiliated
> ungrateful
> animals

With the exception of *animals,* all these words are adult; children may need help in understanding them. They show that the factor of personal time is involved.

Linguistic question 6 can help the teacher see how words cluster into collocations around the once-a-mouse tiger. These words are *handsome, royal, pride, peacocked, lording, offended, humiliated, proud beast, ungrateful.*

Combining linguistic questions 13 and 17 reveals that there are three imperatives, all punctuated with an exclamation mark. Such punctuation suggests that these sentences are pronounced with emphasis or emotion. The first—*Now, imagine the pride of that tiger!*—emphatically includes the readers in the action of the story. The other two—*Go back to the forest and be a mouse again!*—are firm commands by the hermit to the once-a-mouse tiger and emphasize the power of the hermit's magic.

Teaching Plan. After reading the selection with the children, ask them, "What words do you see that are difficult for you to understand? What words do you think are interesting?" Probably they will mention some or all the words you have noted in your linguistic analysis, especially *peacocked* and *lording*. Ask the students, "What is the difference between *peacocks* and *peacocked* in the sentence:

> *The peacocks peacocked around the park?"*

Help them explain in their own words that the *–s* on *peacocks* tells us the number of birds in the park: there were some peacocks. On the other hand, the *–ed* on *peacocked* tells us what the birds were doing in the park. If the children have the words *noun* and *verb* in their vocabulary, encourage them to use these terms. Otherwise let them discuss the ideas in any way that makes sense to them. Then ask, "Does the *–ing* on *lording* in

> *The tiger was lording it over the other animals.*

give the same kind of information about *lording* as the *–ed* does about *peacocked?* Does it say that *lording* is a verb? What verbs ending in *–ing* can be used in the following sentence?"

> He was _____.

The children may think of *walking, dancing, singing, talking,* and many others. The idea that words tell us about themselves by their endings is the point of this discussion. Grammatical terminology is not important; children's comprehension is.

You might also ask the following questions. "Is the story difficult to read? Why?" (Many big words.) "Why does the author use so many big words?" (To make us feel grown-up? To help us learn new words? To tell us that the tiger and hermit are big and important in the story? Other reasons?)

Other questions could concern collocations. Ask, "What words go together to tell us that the once-a-mouse is both a big, important tiger and also a little, unimportant mouse?" (To guide discussion refer to the collocations analyzed in your linguistic analysis.)

In talking about punctuation, say to the children, "Look at the end of the sentences: *Now imagine the pride of that tiger!* and *Go back to the forest and be a mouse again!* What do you see? What marks do you usually find at the end? How is this mark different? What does it mean?" (Emotion, emphasis, and in this case also an order.) The children could probably explain in their own words the idea of requesting or ordering someone to do something. Then ask, "In each sentence who is being ordered? What are they being ordered or requested to do?" The children's answers will reveal their comprehension of the imperative sentences.

As a final step in the lesson, reread the lit bit together, and observe if it has become more meaningful because of the discussion.

Follow-up Evaluation Activities.

1. Students can put together collocations about any idea or object of interest to them. The teacher might suggest ideas such as hobbies, popular people, seasons of the year, holidays, or characters in books. The children could make up stories using their collocations. Point out how the words help to make the story vivid and interesting. Suggest that the children act out their own stories.

2. Students can draw pictures illustrating the different animals in *Once a Mouse.* When the drawings are completed, discuss the mouse's normal size in relation to the larger animals the children drew. Developing a clear conception of relative size is part of a child's intellectual development. Literature can help.

3. Students can interview their parents or grandparents about different names they used for things years ago, such as *ice box* for *refrigerator, undertaker* for *mortician, looking glass* for *mirror.* This activity reinforces the fact that language changes slowly but constantly.

4. Have the students read aloud sentences punctuated with periods. Then ask them to imagine that the period has been changed to an exclamation mark and read the sentence again with an appropriate intonation pattern.

"A Cliché" by Eve Merriam[3]

is what we all say
when we're too lazy
to find another way

and so we say

warm as toast,
quiet as a mouse,
slow as molasses,
quick as a wink.

Think.
Is toast the warmest thing you know?
Think again, it might not be so.
Think again: it might even be snow!
Soft as a lamb's wool, fleecy snow,
a lacy shawl of new-fallen snow.

Listen to that mouse go
scuttling and clawing,
nibbling and pawing.
A mouse can speak
if only a squeak.

Slow as time passes
when you're sad and alone;
quick as an hour can go
happily on your own.

Is a mouse the quietest thing you know?
Think again, it might not be so.
Think again: it might be a shadow.
Quiet as a shadow,
quiet as growing grass,
quiet as a pillow,
or a looking glass.

Slow as molasses,
quick as a wink.
Before you say so,
take time to think.

This poem presents a rather mature stylistic idea—the cliché—and demonstrates that the young child can comprehend abstractions when they are presented concretely in a clear, interesting context. The poem is suitable reading for middle elementary school children, eight and nine years old.

Linguistic Teaching Goals. In teaching this lit bit, the teacher might have several linguistic goals. The first would be to teach students not only to understand comparisons but also to use them in individual, fresh ways so as to avoid clichés. The next goal would be to help children comprehend three aspects of grammar by using them in concrete and easily grasped contexts: factual and evaluative adjectives, definite and indefinite articles, commands and requests.

Linguistic Analysis. The following linguistic questions focus the teacher's linguistic analysis.

1. **What are the unusual words and what do they mean in this context? What other meanings for them do you know? What synonyms could be substituted for them in this context?**
7. **What is the proportion of factual to evaluative adjectives? How does it affect the tone of the selection?**
8. **What comparisons are used? Are any of them clichés? How do the comparisons strengthen or weaken the literary selection?**
11. **How frequent is the definite article** the **as opposed to the indefinite article** a (an)**? How does the frequency reflect the author's relationship to the reader?**
13. **How frequently are imperatives, with or without** you**, expressed? What reasons might explain their use in this context?**

Using linguistic question 1, note that probably two expressions are unfamiliar to the students: cliché and looking glass. Cliché is excellently defined by the poem itself as a worn-out comparison, and looking glass can easily be defined as "mirror." If the children are acquainted with Lewis Carroll's Through the Looking Glass, they will have no problem with the expression here.

Using linguistic question 7, the teacher can list all the adjectives in the poem:

lazy	1 use	soft	1 use
warm (est)	2 uses	fleecy	1 use
quiet (est)	5 uses	lacy	1 use
slow	3 uses	sad	1 use
quick	3 uses	alone	1 use

In the context of the poem, all these adjectives seem to be factual rather than evaluative. Thus the poem seems close to actual living, referring to facts that the children will recognize.

Using linguistic question 8, observe that one type of adverbialization—the one with the signal word *as*—appears in the poem to illustrate the idea of comparison, which is vital to the context. Another type of comparison uses the signal word *like*, as in

His voice sounded *like* a drum.
The road stretches out *like* a snake.

In the poem four comparisons are labeled "clichés" and are identified as such by being printed in italics:

warm as toast
quiet as a mouse
slow as molasses
quick as a wink.

All these clichés have the same grammatical structure:

adjective + *as* + noun

This structure is easy for children to understand and imitate. Therefore they can demonstrate their underlying understanding of grammar without talking about grammatical abstractions.

Using linguistic question 11, count and classify the occurrences of the articles. Counting the title there are thirteen uses of the indefinite article *a* and only two uses of the definite article *the*. Both of these appear in two sentences of similar structure:

Is toast *the* warmest thing you know?
Is the mouse *the* quietest thing you know?

These two sentences ask the reader to *think with* the writer about things they both know, their shared knowledge. The definite article subtly and pleasantly emphasizes the bond of understanding which they share as thinking human beings.

Using linguistic question 13, count the imperatives in the poem. There are seven: five *thinks*, one *listen*, and one *take time to think*. In each of these imperatives the author orders the reader to think about the real world, to look and listen with fresh, open eyes and ears, and not to accept automatically the tired words of other people.

Teaching Plan. Start by reading the poem aloud to the children as they read along silently with you. Explain in passing that *looking glass* means "mirror." Note the italics in which the clichés are printed in the poem.

Ask the children, "When I say, 'John is as loud as a fog horn', what am I saying? Do I mean that he is a fog horn?" (No, he has a very loud voice. I am comparing his loud voice to something else loud.) "What is meant by *warm as toast*? What other comparisons can you think of instead of *warm as toast*?" The poet suggests *warm as snow*. That comparison is unusual because we usually think of snow as cold, not warm. The poet helps us understand how snow can be thought of as warm. It is soft as lamb's wool making a fleecy, lacy shawl. Wool and shawls are warm. Therefore, the comparison has truth in it and we feel that is effective; it works. "What comparisons does the poet suggest instead of *as quiet as a mouse*?" (A shadow, growing grass, a pillow, a mirror.) Have the children make up their own explanations about why these comparisons are effective. "What other comparisons can you suggest?" Encourage creativity; accept all suggestions. Then try inventing new comparisons for *slow as molasses* and *quick as a wink*.

Tell the children about the other kind of comparison, which uses *like* instead of *as*, and give several examples. Children understand comparisons and enjoy reading and creating them. Kenneth Koch's *Wishes, Lies and Dreams* (pp. 87–106) has many examples written by children in grades 1 through 6.

In the course of the discussion, point out that words like *warm, quiet, slow,* and *quick* are called "adjectives." Ask "Do these words state facts or tell the poet's opinion? Think of adjectives that are in other clichés you know." (*Busy as a bee, bright as a button, brown as a berry, blue as the sky, red as a rose.*) Working with the children, you make a chart with the clichés in one column and fresh, new comparisons in another parallel column.

Ask the children, "Why do you think the poet wrote this poem?" (To get the reader to think.) "What does she order us, the readers, to do?" Help the children find the imperatives in the poem that reinforce the idea of ordering the reader to make fresh, new comparisons instead of automatically using the familiar cliché.

As a final step in the lesson, reread the poem with the children to discover if it is more meaningful because of your linguistically oriented teaching.

Follow-up Evaluation Activities.

1. Hold up something quite ordinary (like an apple, a shoe, or a piece of paper), and ask the children to create as many fresh, new comparisons as they can imagine. Encourage the children to use both the *as* and *like* forms of comparison.

2. Arranged in groups, the children can work together in writing their own new comparisons. These can be illustrated, read aloud to the class, and posted on a bulletin board or bound into a volume.

3. Suggest specifically that the children use factual and evaluative adjectives in their comparisons to reveal how well they understand the difference. These adjectives can be discussed to see if one or the other type is easier to write. Examples of factual adjectives might refer, for example to colors: red as ____ , green as ____ ; evaluative adjectives might refer to feelings: *wonderful as* ____ , *interesting as* ____ . In each case the comparison should not be a cliché.

4. Suggest frames like *the racers ran like* ____ or *those birds are singing like* ____ , and ask students to make fresh, new comparisons of the *like* type from them, again avoiding clichés. Here and in the preceding activity, expect some differences of opinion on what a cliché actually is. The children

may not agree with the teacher because of age and experience difference.

"Arithmetic" by Carl Sandburg[4]

Arithmetic is where numbers fly like pigeons in and out of your head.

Arithmetic tells you how many you lose or win if you know how many you had before you lost or won.

Arithmetic is seven eleven all good children go to heaven—or five six bundle of sticks.

Arithmetic is numbers you squeeze from your head to your hand to your pencil to your paper till you get the answer.

Arithmetic is where the answer is right and everything is nice and you can look out of the window and see the blue sky—or the answer is wrong and you have to start all over and try again and see how it comes out this time.

If you take a number and double it and double it again and then double it a few more times, the number gets bigger and bigger and goes higher and higher and only arithmetic can tell you what the number is when you decide to quit doubling.

Arithmetic is where you have to multiply—and you carry the multiplication table in your head and hope you won't lose it.

If you have two animal crackers, one good and one bad, and you eat one and a striped zebra with streaks all over him eats the other, how many animal crackers will you have if somebody offers you five six seven and you say No no no and you say Nay nay nay and you say Nix nix nix?

If you ask your mother for one fried egg for breakfast and she gives you two fried eggs and you eat both of them, who is better in arithmetic, you or your mother?

Carl Sandburg's poem "Arithmetic" describes a child's–eye view of a school subject that often demands thought more abstract than young children can achieve easily. This lit bit ties literature and math together and shows students coping with abstractions. The poem is suitable for later elementary children, aged ten and eleven.

Linguistic Teaching Goals. In presenting this lit bit, the teacher might have two linguistic goals. One could be to help students understand that writers choose words skillfully to reinforce and clarify their ideas. The second linguistic goal could be to help students learn that changes in intonation affect meaning.

Linguistic Analysis. The following linguistic questions focus the teacher's linguistic analysis.

4. What is the author's policy about repeating words as contrasted with using a variety of synonyms? What are the advantages and/or disadvantages of repetition?

7. What is the proportion of factual to evaluative adjectives? How does it affect the tone of the selection?

11. How frequent is the definite article the as opposed to the indefinite article a (an)? How does the frequency reflect the author's relationship to the reader?

15. How could a change in intonation change the meaning of a particular word or sentence in the selection?

Using linguistic question 4, observe that the most frequently used words are you and your. Counted together, they total thirty-four occurrences. The word arithmetic occurs eight times. These words refer to the two central ideas of the poem and their relationship to each other. The repetition of the word number three times reinforces this conclusion. The poem makes nine statements, and in six of them the word arithmetic stands in the important position of first word in the sentence. Moreover, in four of the nine statements, the subordinator if appears, marking a very common form of a typical arithmetic problem.

Using linguistic question 11, note that there are eight instances of the definite article the in the poem. Therefore the writer seems to be suggesting that we are talking about well-known, familiar objects and ideas which are present in everybody's experience.

Using linguistiic question 7, analyze the poem's adjectives. Factual adjectives seem to be the following: blue, right, wrong, bigger (twice), and higher (twice). Evaluative adjectives seem to be these: good (twice), nice, better, and bad. They all concern abstract qualities of goodness or badness. Thus the factual adjectives predominate over the evaluative.

Applying linguistic question 15, the two following sentences will seem interesting.

1. "Arithmetic is seven eleven all good children go to heaven—or five six bundle of sticks."
2. "If you ask your mother for one fried egg for breakfast and she gives you two fried eggs and you eat both of them, who is better in arithmetic, you or your mother?"

The first sentence could be said normally or it could be said with the singsong intonation of the counting rhyme used by very young children when learning to count or by older children when bouncing balls. The second sentence could be read with a drop in pitch at the end on the word *mother*, or with a rise in pitch there. The second intonation pattern will imply, "You don't really mean anything as silly as that, do you?"

Teaching Plan. After reading the poem aloud while the students read along silently, ask them to count repetitions of different words. When the children discover the frequency of *arithmetic, you* and *yours*, and the definite article *the*, explore the possible meanings of their findings with them. Certainly, the author wishes to emphasize the ideas which these words represent, implying that you and arithmetic are closely related. The definite article adds the information that this relationship is clear and well known. Other patterns of words underscore the writer's ideas about arithmetic by repetition of the word *number* (along with actual names of numbers, counting rhyme patterns, and *if*–clause, math–problem patterns). Help the students comprehend these and other ideas stimulated by the poem, with the basic objective of leading them to realize that skillful writers make their language reinforce and clarify their points.

Examine the adjectives so that the students can see that authors use adjectives to express not only their ideas but also their feelings. Suggest that the students find the adjectives in the poem and classify them as facts or feelings. In small groups, the students could discuss what the author's feelings about arithmetic really are and how they match or differ from their own feelings.

Experimenting with changing intonation patterns is another interesting activity to help students understand that a poem may communicate more than one meaning, depending on how it is spoken or read.

As a final step in the lesson, reread the poem with the children to discover if it is more meaningful because of your linguistically oriented teaching.

Follow-up Evaluation Activities.

1. Several students can tape-record their readings of the poem. When the recording is played, discuss the interesting differences.
2. Students can work together in groups to prepare a description of a learning process other than arithmetic. It could be a school subject like social studies or science, or it could be a game or hobby like skateboarding or checkers. Their descriptions might spark a lively discussion.
3. Ask the students to volunteer to say ordinary sentences such as

> *What are you doing?*
> *Please help me now.*
> *You're out.*

in several different ways to communicate various meanings. Their classmates can try to guess each meaning and who might use it.

From *The Hobbit* by J. R. R. Tolkien[5]

Three very large persons sitting round a very large fire of beech-logs. They were toasting mutton on long spits of wood, and licking the gravy off their fingers. There was a fine toothsome smell. Also there was a barrel of good drink at hand, and they were drinking out of jugs. But they were trolls. Obviously trolls. Even Bilbo, in spite of his sheltered life, could see that: from the great heavy faces of them, and their size, and the shape of their legs, not to mention their language, which was not drawing-room fashion at all, at all.

"Mutton yesterday, mutton today, and blimey, if it don't look like mutton again tomorrer," said one of the trolls.

"Never a blinking bit of manflesh have we had for long enough," said a second. "What the 'ell William was a–thinkin' of to bring us into these parts at all, beats me—and the drink runnin' short, what's more," he said jogging the elbow of William, who was taking a pull at his jug.

William choked, "Shut yer mouth!" he said as soon as he could. "Yer can't expect folk to stop here for ever just to be et by you and Bert. You've et a village and a half between yer, since we come down from the mountains. How much more d'yer want? And time's been up our way, when yer'd have said 'thank yer Bill' for a nice bit o'fat valley mutton like what this is." He took a big bite off a sheep's leg he was toasting, and wiped his lips on his sleeve.

This lit bit describes the trolls who inhabit the fantastic "Middle Earth" of J. R. R. Tolkien, author of *The Hobbit*. He was an Englishman, a retired professor from Oxford University, as well as an expert on the folktales and myths of northwest Europe. Therefore the language of *The Hobbit* differs from characteristic American English. This lit bit is appropriate reading for later elementary or middle school students, aged eleven and twelve.

Linguistic Teaching Goals. In presenting this lit bit, the teacher might have three linguistic goals. The first might emphasize the importance of time in language and literature. The second could be to explain some uses of dialects in literature. The third might be to point out that we can use various types of sentences in speaking and writing.

Linguistic Analysis. The following linguistic questions focus the teacher's linguistic analysis.

1. **What are the unusual words and what do they mean in this context? What other meanings for them do you know? What synonyms could be substituted for them in this context?**
6. **Which words cluster into collocations to emphasize various ideas in the selection?**
9. **How frequently are regional and/or social dialect markers used? What reasons might the author have for using dialects and how valid are these reasons?**

12. What is the distribution of sentence types: fragments, basic sentences, sentences with joining transforms, inserting transforms, or both? How does this distribution affect the reading ease or difficulty of the selection?

14. If the word order is inverted, how can it be rearranged into normal, Modern English? What reasons might explain its inversion and how valid are these reasons?

16. How powerfully do verbs carry meaning without adjectives or manner adverbs to help them?

Using linguistic question 1, note that the students may need explanations of the following words:

toasting—here a synonym for roasting;
mutton—flesh of a mature sheep, used as food;
toothsome—having a tasty flavor and a pleasing texture;
trolls—in Teutonic folklore, either dwarfs or giants— here clearly giants;
drawing room—formal reception room;
manflesh—flesh of a man;
jogging—shaking or slightly pushing.

Using linguistic question 6, observe the collocations clustered around the ideas of: (1) food and drink, and (2) trolls.

Food and drink collocation

mutton	5 uses	toasting	1 use	gravy	1 use
drinking	1 use	big bite	1 use	jug(s)	2 uses
				licking	1 use

Troll collocation

very large	1 use	great, heavy faces	1 use
barrel	1 use	big bite of sheep's leg	1 use
long spits	1 use	bigness of trolls	1 use
jug(s)	2 uses	et village and a half	1 use

Using linguistic question 9, note that there is some British regional dialect (et, blimey, blinking, jug) and a few social dialect items like *it don't look like mutton again tomorrer* and *a–thinkin'*.

Using linguistic question 12, examine the sentence types in the selection. There are two fragments: *Three very large persons sitting round a very large fire of beech-logs* and *Obviously trolls*. There are only two basic sentences, one transformed into a WH–question. They are *But they were trolls* and *How much more d'yer want?* There are no sentences with only joining transforms. Most of the sentences are much more complicated: sentences joined together and inserted one into another.

Using linguistic question 14, observe that two sentences show inverted word order. One is the WH–question cited above. The other is *Never a blinking bit of manflesh have we had for long enough*. Normal word order would be *We have never had a blinking bit of manflesh for long enough*. When the author puts the *never* part of the sentence first, he emphasizes the sad monotony of the trolls' steady diet of mutton.

Using linguistic question 16, note that there are many verbs in the selection but no manner adverbs or adjectives to help carry their meaning. This fact suggests that Tolkien recognizes the importance of making every word use as much power as possible. The following is a list of these powerful verbs.

toasting mutton	licking gravy	drinking out of jugs
beats me	jogging the elbow	taking a pull at the jug
choked	shut your mouth wiped his lips	et a village

Teaching Plan. After reading the lit bit aloud with the children, briefly explain the meanings of the unusual words. Then consider the following questions with the students. "Why does the word *toasting* seem strange in connection with the word *mutton?*" (We toast marshmallows, which cook much more quickly and easily than mutton, a tough meat.) Point out that in the United States butchers sell lamb, the flesh of young sheep, more commonly than mutton, the flesh of mature sheep. In England mutton is much more common. Tolkien's use of *mutton* reflects British background and dialect. The word *toothsome* is probably unfamiliar for different reasons: it is literary and old-fashioned. In the lit bit it is appropriate because it neatly combines appeals to the sense of taste and sight. "The word *trolls* can mean either dwarfs or giants. Which use is intended here?" About the word *drawing-room*, after defining it as "a large reception hall," ask the children how drawing-room language would differ from the trolls' language. (Drawing-room language would much more dignified and polite.) Concerning the word *manflesh*, point out that the word is not in dictionaries but is made by putting two other words together to make one new one. English constantly makes new words in this way. (*Spaceship, softland,* and *skyway* are three other examples.)

Explain the inverted *never* sentence by rearranging its word order. Ask the children why they think Tolkien used the unusual arrangement of words in this sentence.

Discuss collocations, asking students to find all the words clustering around the ideas of food-and-drink or trolls.

As a final step in the lesson, reread the lit bit with the children to unify their comprehension of its meaning, noting if the passage has been enriched as a result of your linguistic teaching plan.

Follow-up Evaluation Activities.

1. Encourage the students to read other parts of *The Hobbit* so they become acquainted with hobbits, dwarfs, and elves, as well as trolls. Suggest that the students invent their own fantasy stories, using these or other fanciful characters. In this connection, students could read and write about *The Gammage Cup* by Carol Kendall (New York: Harcourt Brace Jovanovich, 1959). This fantasy story from the United States, tells about the lives and adventures of the Minnipins, who could be contrasted with Tolkien's little people.

2. Students can try putting Tolkien's sentences together in different sentence patterns. Class discussion could focus on how the changed patterns affect the style of the lit bit and the reader's sense of enjoying it.

3. Have the students create new words like *manflesh* by combining two words. Ask the children to explain the meanings of their new words.

SUGGESTIONS FOR DISCUSSION AND STUDY

1. Select two other lit bits—one prose and one poetry—and practice applying the procedures described in this chapter. Share your results with your classmates. What additional suggestions do they offer to extend or deepen your linguistic analysis and teaching plan?

2. What new dimensions do the linguistic questions add to the usual "comprehension questions" offered in traditional literature textbooks? Copy a set of comprehension questions and add linguistic insights to improve or clarify them.

3. It is usually agreed that the chief value and purpose of analysis is to achieve better synthesis. How is this truth recognized in the teaching plans for the lit bits analyzed in this chapter?

4. An important educational principle is that the success of stated teaching goals should be evaluated in the course of, or at the end of, the lesson or unit. Too often grandiose goals are stated at the outset and then completely disregarded or forgotten. One important evaluative criterion is teachers' subjective judgments on their own success, but additional, more objective criteria are also necessary. Check your own lit bits to be sure that your evaluative follow-up activities test your linguistic teaching goals.

5. Prepare a reference list of lit bits that you could effectively use with linguistic questions to enhance your students' comprehension of literature.

6. Compile a list of lit bits using various dialects. Refer to this list during a unit on dialects.

7. Why should teaching plans differ for students at different stages of development? Contrast several teaching plans for various grade levels.

NOTES

[1] (New York: Coward McCann, 1928), unpaged, first five pages of text.

[2] (New York: Charles Scribner's Sons, 1961), unpaged, last fifteen pages of text.

[3] *It Doesn't Always Have to Rhyme* (New York: Atheneum, 1971), pp. 48–50.

[4] *The Complete Poems of Carl Sandburg* (New York: Harcourt Brace Jovanovich, 1969, 1970), pp. 655–656.

[5] (New York: Ballantine Books, 1937, 1938), p. 46.

8

Applying Linguistics to Teaching Writing

OVERVIEW AND PURPOSE OF THE CHAPTER

In learning to write, young children must discover how writing, which is new to them, differs from speaking, which they learned out of consciousness before entering school. One important difference is that writers have no listeners to give them feedback, to make encouraging noises and/or helpful gestures signaling their attention and understanding. The pitches, stresses, and pauses of intonation, as well as the movements and facial expressions of body language help speakers know how effectively they are communicating with their listeners. Writers have only a few imperfect ways to represent these rich speech signals. Punctuation marks, capital letters, and paragraphs are the weak reflections of the strong signals of speech.

Children normally begin writing by trying to write down their own speech. However, this is a more complicated process than we adults remember. Children must listen to what they would say if they were speaking and then try to represent it in writing. In other words, they have to hear and somehow analyze their speech before recording it. Recording speech means controlling the handwriting and spelling systems and also figuring out where words start and stop. In speech, words often run together into meaningful groups. For example, *drinkapintamilkaday* gives beginning writers no accurate information as to where to put white space to divide the written words. Thus children cannot use speech as a dependable model for writing.

Nonstandard–speaking children have special difficulties in learning to write. Traditionally, writing has been linked to reading, which is usually written in standard written English (as we have seen in discussing reading). Nonstandard speakers are expected to perform a more difficult feat of learning than are their peers who speak standard spoken English. They must first translate their speech into standard written English and then transcribe it.

Another difference between speaking and writing is that writing is a less tolerant mode of communication than speech. When we speak we can make slips of the tongue, errors in agreement, hesitations, repetitions, and revisions without anyone really noticing. However, writing demands forward planning and careful attention to the organization of ideas as well as to punctuation, spelling, capitalization, and other mechanics of graphic representation. From this point of view, writing is indeed a strictly intolerant mode of communication.

From another viewpoint, however, writing has its own virtues. It helps children use language in new ways. Since writing requires more planning, it develops the ability to use language for thinking and to organize what we have to say. It helps us to predict our readers' reactions and to modify our writing in the light of those predictions. On the whole, mature writing is more demanding, more elaborate, and more complete than mature speech.

However, mature writing is very different from beginning writing. Teachers can easily distinguish between the compositions of a third grader and a sixth grader. The older student would use a better vocabulary, longer sentences, and a larger proportion of sentences with insertions.

In the early 1960s Kellogg Hunt began research to define objectively our intuitive judgments about writing maturity.[1] He analyzed samples of writing by fourth, eighth, and twelfth graders and adult professional writers. Shortly thereafter, Roy O'Donnell, William Griffin, and Raymond Norris made similar analyses of the sentence structure of the speech of children in the first, second, and third grades and the writing of fifth and seventh graders.[2] From these studies we have a comprehensive spread of information on the sentence structure of young school children. The research clearly shows that throughout school and beyond, writers progressively complicate their sentence structure in specific, systematic ways.

In his research Hunt defined a new unit of measurement—the minimal terminable unit, or T–unit, for short—to demonstrate that structure, not length, was the crucial signal of growth toward syntactic maturity. In fact, very young children often utter extremely long sentences, all strung together by *ands*. Hunt's T–unit is one main clause plus whatever subordinate clauses are joined to or inserted into it. Hunt defines a *clause* as a group of words with one subject or one set of coordinate subjects with one verb phrase or one set of coordinated verb phrases. Thus, *Karl left the party* is one clause as is *Karl and Marie left the party and went home.*

To demonstrate the usefulness of the T–unit, Hunt quoted a theme written by a fourth grader. Its only punctuation was a period at the end. Its length of sixty-four words would make it much more syntactically mature than the sentences of adult professional writers. However, when the theme was divided into T–units, their word count averaged 11.34 words per T–unit, approximately the syntactic maturity of an eighth grader. The T–unit has proved to be the most accurate measure of syntactic maturity yet discovered.

Teachers' linguistic knowledge of joining and inserting transformations helps them understand and apply this research to their students' development toward syntactic maturity. Children often write sentences like *There is a clown in the park and the clown is my friend.* It consists of two T–units of seven and five words respectively tied together with the conjunction *and.* A more syntactically mature writer would probably use an adjectivalization and write *There is a clown in the park who is my friend.* Although the sentence is two words shorter, it contains one T–unit eleven words long, a clear example that T–unit length is a more accurate index to syntactic maturity than is sentence length. Children can easily master these linguistic insights if the teacher demonstrates them by many clear and interesting examples.

Adjectivalizations are important for another reason. As was noted in the discussion of them in chapter 3, adjectivalizations can be further shortened by omitting other words in the insert. Thus they help create sentences that are shorter but more concise and mature.

Adverbializations and nominalizations also appear frequently in beginning writing as children develop into more mature writers. The use of these insertions greatly depends on what subject is being discussed, and how.

These linguistic insights from transformational grammar have triggered a new method of relating grammar to writing—sentence combining. The next section of this chapter will discuss sentence combining in detail. Several insights on teaching punctuation are implicit in the discussion.

The final section of the chapter will deal with the teaching of spelling. It draws many insights from psycholinguistics and applies them to the teaching of writing.

Once again, remember that no formal abstract grammar teaching should be inflicted upon young school children. It is a waste of time until they are mature enough to understand it.

SENTENCE COMBINING

In the late 1960s and early 1970s John Mellon[3] and Frank O'Hare[4]—basing their work on Hunt's findings—demonstrated that when students systematically practiced putting short sentences together in patterned ways to make longer sentences, those students' rate of growth toward syntactic maturity was speeded up. Their rate became twice that which Hunt had defined as normal. Thus, sentence–combining exercises give teachers opportunities to use their comprehension of insertion transformations to accelerate their students' growth in writing mature sentences.

Traditionally it was assumed, implicitly or explicitly, that teaching grammar improved writing. Yet no research has ever supported this assumption. Instead, formal, abstract grammar teaching may even have had a harmful effect if it displaced practice in actual writing. Hence the affirmative results of sentence–combining exercises was a true breakthrough. Teachers can present these exercises casually as a gamelike activity. Students quickly understand the idea and enjoy using it while they grow steadily toward syntactic maturity.

Using Joining Transformations

The conjunction *and* is the key to creating joining transforms. Its use is early and frequent in children's speech and appears immediately when they start to write.

In sentence–combining exercises children can be given pairs of short sentences and asked to put them together by using *and*.

> Karen seemed happy. Kevin seemed glad.
> Karen seemed happy and Kevin seemed glad.

Adding more sentences is easy.

> Karen seemed happy and Kevin seemed glad and Kelly seemed surprised and Karl seemed pleased.

As long as each sentence has its own separate subject noun phrase and separate predicate verb phrase, the process can continue indefinitely.

However, as soon as there is overlapping of any part of the separate sentence, the *and* acts like an eraser and removes the repetition. Consider this set of sentences.

> Karen seemed happy. Kevin seemed happy.

The subject noun phrases—*Karen* and *Kevin*—are the only different words in the two sentences. The two sentences can be joined by *and*, which erases the repetition: *seemed happy*.

> Karen and Kevin seemed happy.

If we join the following sentences:

> Karen seemed happy. Karen seemed glad.

the difference is in the predicate adjectives—*happy* and *glad*. Notice that again the *and* erases the repeated *Karen seemed*:

Karen seemed happy and glad.

Joining transformations can teach children a rule about punctuating a series. Assume that these four sentences are to be joined by *and*:

At the supermarket Mrs. Clancy bought bread.
At the supermarket Mrs. Clancy bought milk.
At the supermarket Mrs. Clancy bought meat.
At the supermarket Mrs. Clancy bought fruit.

Drawing on what they have learned, the children might join the sentence to produce:

At the supermarket Mrs. Clancy bought bread and milk and meat and fruit.

Although this sentence is completely grammatical, the writer has the option of replacing the first two *and*s by commas, and may or may not use a comma before the last *and*, as preferred.

At the supermarket Mrs. Clancy bought break, milk, meat, and fruit.

Thus a shorter sentence is created, and such economy in expression is generally considered a stylistic virtue.

One of the important side effects of sentence—combining exercises is that students become aware of stylistic options in writing. That is, they learn that there is always more than one way to express any idea.

Using Insertion Transformations

Young children use one type of nominal insert very fluently in speech. In reporting a conversation or in telling a story, children often use *that* + sentence nominal inserts. These follow verbs that express saying, thinking, or knowing, and they can be of two forms:

1. Jack said (that) he was going to climb the beanstalk.
2. Jack said, "I am going to climb the beanstalk."

With the teacher's help, sentences such as the second can be used to teach children how to punctuate direct quotations. The two sentences can be combined as follows:

> Jack said [＿＿＿＿＿＿]
> I am going to climb the beanstalk.

The combination reveals how pronouns and verbs change when they move from direct to indirect quotation. That is, *I* becomes *he*, and *am* becomes *was*.

Here is another pair of sentences, illustrating another verb of saying:

> Little Red Riding Hood's mother told her [＿＿＿＿＿＿＿]
> Take the basket to Grandmother.

These can combine in either of two ways:

> Little Red Riding Hood's mother told her that she should take the basket to Grandmother.
> Little Red Riding Hood's mother told her, "Take the basket to Grandmother."

Note that the sentence about Red Riding Hood could also use an infinitive nominal insert:

> Little Red Riding Hood's mother told her to take the basket to Grandmother.

Again the different stylistic options available can be pointed out to students. There is no one correct way to put the sentences together. It depends on the wishes of the writer.

In the same way, WH–word nominal inserts can follow verbs of asking:

> The three bears asked [＿＿＿＿＿＿]
> Who is in our house?

The result sentence will read as either of the following sentences.

> The three bears asked who was in their house.
> The three bears asked. "Who is in our house?"

Again, practical teaching of punctuation can develop naturally from the use of the question mark as it appears in inserts. This knowledge can be added to the students' previous knowledge of how question marks are used in writing.

Children can easily practice adjectivalization by combining sentences like the following. In them, succeeding sentences share nouns; the sentences are put together and repetition is removed—all without changing the underlying meaning of the sentences. In this example five sentences are inserted into one receiver:

> Receiver: She was the witch.
> Inserts: The witch was evil.
> The witch was old.
> The witch lived in the mountains.
> The mountains are high.
> The mountains are on the other side of the world.
> Result: She was the evil old witch who lived in the high mountains on the other side of the world.

Children can also practice adverbializations, using subordinators to put the sentences together.

> Receiver: The rain fell steadily.
> Insert: (because) It was April.
> Result: The rain fell steadily because it was April.

> Receiver: Jack answered the phone.
> Insert: (when) His father called him.
> Result: Jack answered the phone when his father called him.

> Receiver: Betty had a CB radio.
> Insert: (although) She did not listen to it.
> Result: Betty had a CB radio although she did not listen to it.

Other sets of sentences can be combined by putting together more than one type of insertion. For example, nominalization, adjectivalization, adverbialization, and joining can all be used in combining the following sentences.

Receiver: Pam was looking forward to [   ]
Inserts: Pam would meet the girl.
   The girl was new.
   The girl lived on the block.
   (and) The girl has moved from Cleveland.
   (before) School began.
Result: Pam was looking forward to meeting the new
   girl who lived on the block and who had moved from
   Cleveland before school began.

Sentence–combining exercises can be either structured or unstructured. That is, the students can be given a pattern to follow and signals to guide them through it (as in the examples above). Or they can be given sets of sentences and asked to put them together in any way they wish, as long as they keep the same general meaning. For example, here is a group of sentences about a picnic:

Our class is planning a picnic.
The picnic will be at Lake Crystal.
Lake Crystal is a lake near our school.
Lake Crystal is clear.
Lake Crystal is blue.

An adult would probably combine these sentences into one long sentence like

Our class is planning a picnic at Lake Crystal, a clear, blue lake near our school.

Children of different ages will make other, different combinations. As long as they create sentences, not sentence fragments, the teacher should accept all options. It can become a game to see how many different combinations students can make.

SPELLING

Many preschool children invent their own spellings for words that they have in their speaking vocabulary. Their invented spellings show how they organize and classify sounds they hear.[5] They use this system until it is replaced by the standard spelling system after they enter school.

Apparently, children who invent their own spelling system already know their A–B–Cs, the traditional names for the letters of the alphabet. Then they learn that a letter may spell a sound of its name. For example, the "long a" /ey/ of *name* is spelled with the letter *a*. Children try to extend this principle to spell all the words in their speaking vocabulary but soon discover that the twenty-six letters of the alphabet are not enough to spell all words because English has more than twenty-six speech sounds, or phonemes. At this point the children either ask adults how to spell the missing sounds or they invent their own nonstandard spelling system, which shows how the children hear and organize sounds. They do not use letters without plan or pattern. Their guesses are reasoned miscues that are windows into their minds. After they enter school, they learn that their guesses do not necessarily match the standard spelling system of English.

In discussing the teaching of spelling, Carol Chomsky says, "Good spellers, children and adults alike, recognize that related words are spelled alike even though they are pronounced differently. They seem to rely on an underlying picture of the words that is independent of its varying pronunciations."[6] The English spelling system reflects the underlying abstract meaning, while the English pronunciation system provides the sounds to be spoken.

For example, the rules of pronunciation tell us that the sounds of words change as the position of the word stress changes. Compare the sounds of the vowels in these three related words:

photograph	photography	photographic
/fówtəgræf/	/fətɔ́grəfiy/	/fowtəgrǽfik/

In spite of their surface differences in pronunciation, they all have the same underlying meaning: image produced on a sensitivized surface by the action of radiant energy. We cannot spell our mental picture of this meaning without using the concrete visible letters *p–h–o–t–o–g–r–a–p–h*. Our spelling rules hold these letters constant and firm even while our pronunciation rules guide us to different sounds for their vowels.

Consonants, too, obey similar spelling rules, which hold underlying roots constant and firm even while the pronunciation rules demand differing pronunciations. Here are several interesting illustrations. In each pair the abstract root is spelled identically but pronounced differently.

sign	signal	right	righteous
bomb	bombard	soft	soften

On the other hand, spelling often separates homonyms by recording the differences in meaning beneath the surface sound-alikes. That is, the words are spelled differently even though they sound the same. For example, just as spelling ties *right* and *righteous* together, it also separates *right* from its three homonyms: *rite*, *write*, and *wright*.

Probably the most important function of the linguistically oriented spelling teacher is to alert students to as much of the spelling system as they are mature enough to understand. This help is very different from giving students so-called "memory jogs" for remembering "spelling demons." The memory jog that works for one person may not work for another. For example, take the memory jog: "*i* before *e* except after *c*." Memorizing this jingle does not guarantee the correct spelling of *believe* and *receive*; and, besides, the memory jog has exceptions that may make the student distrust the validity of the system.

Carol Chomsky suggests a number of spelling lessons based on linguistic insights.[7] These exercises can also serve as vocabulary builders.

1. Give children a list of words with a /ə/ vowel omitted and ask them to think of a related word that gives them a clear clue to the spelling. The clue turns out to be the same one which preschool children used in inventing their own spelling system as they applied their knowledge of the names of the letters in the traditional A–B–Cs.

(1)	(2)
pres__dent	(preside)
prec__dent	(precede)
comp__sition	(compose)
imm__grate	(migrate)
janit__r	(janitorial)
maj__r	(majority)
comp__rable	(compare)

Or just give column (2) and ask the children to think of other forms of the word and notice how vowel sounds shift around. The more inventive the teacher can be in helping children think of related words, the better.

2. Help the students guess the correct consonant when two or more seem possible. In column (1) the spelling is ambiguous. The related word in column (2) gives the key to the correct choice.

(1)	(2)
criticize (c, s)	critical
medicine (c, s)	medical
nation (t, sh)	native
gradual (d, j)	grade
racial (t, c, sh)	race
righteous (t, ch)	right

Again the teacher can plan helpful hints to stimulate the children's inventiveness.

3. Help the children observe silent consonants by matching them to related words where the consonants are not silent.

(1)	(2)
muscle	muscular
sign	signal
bomb	bombard
soften	soft

Exercises like these show the learner that spelling often corresponds to something already known. Spelling is not random, without system or pattern. Teachers should work with children to find ways to help them learn words frequently misspelled, trying to discover relationships wherever they exist. Knowledge of dialects helps here. For example, nonstandard black English speakers have many homonyms that standard speakers lack (as discussed in chapter 5). Hence these children must memorize the spelling of many words which speakers of other dialects hear as different.

Sometimes unusual spellings can be explained by reference to their history. As we saw in chapter 4, English has borrowed many words from foreign languages as it has met those languages in its spread through trade, exploration, and colonization. Usually borrowed words are adopted into English without changing their foreign spelling. Some examples are *bourgeois* from French, *disciple* from Latin, *chaos* from Greek, *patio* from Spanish, and *sauerkraut* from German. The spellings of these words have to be memorized as separate items.

The objective of the linguistically informed spelling teacher is to make children aware at every step of their development that the spelling system is regular. Certainly, teachers must choose words and ideas within the students' understanding. For example, young children cannot be expected to use the word *malignant* to help them guess the spelling of the word *malign*. Nor can they associate *critical* with *criticize* to guess that the /s/ sound in criticize is spelled with a *c*. However, as children mature, their command of the "big words" of the "learned vocabulary" increases. Their reading of literature and their study of language are two powerful sources for this increase.

As practical teachers, we realize that our generalizations cannot solve all problems in teaching spelling. Nevertheless, these generalizations convince us that spelling is systematically related to sounds, a fact that many teachers do not believe or use. Because the relationships are more complex than traditional rules state, linguistic insights are useful.

SUGGESTIONS FOR STUDY AND DISCUSSION

1. Explain why a large number of words per T–unit would show greater syntactic maturity than a large number of words per sentence.

2. The following samples were produced in a study by Kellogg Hunt, reported in *Syntactic Maturity in Schoolchildren and Adults*.[8] He gave fourth, eighth, twelfth graders, and skilled adults the same set of very short sentences— which he called "kernels"—and asked them to rewrite them "in a better way." Read the kernels first and then the four ver-

sions that follow. By studying the four versions, decide which was written by a typical member of each group of writers, and explain your decisions.

Kernels

Aluminum is a metal.
It is abundant.
It has many uses.
It comes from bauxite.
Bauxite is an ore.
Bauxite looks like clay.
They grind the bauxite.
It contains several other substances.
Pressure is in the tanks.

Version a: Aluminum is an abundant metal, has many uses, and comes from bauxite which is an ore that looks like clay. Bauxite contains several other substances. Workmen extract these from bauxite by grinding it, then putting it in pressure tanks . . .

Version b: Aluminum, an abundant metal of many uses, is obtained from bauxite, a clay-like ore. To extract the other substances found in bauxite the ore is ground and put in pressure tanks.

Version c: Aluminum is a metal and is abundant. It has many uses and it comes from bauxite. Bauxite is an ore and bauxite looks like clay. Bauxite contains aluminum and it contains several other substances. Workmen extract these other substances from the bauxite. They grind the bauxite and put it in tanks. Pressure is in the tanks . . .

Version d: Aluminum is an abundant metal with many uses. It comes from an ore called bauxite that looks like clay. It contains aluminum and several other substances which are extracted from the bauxite. They grind the bauxite and put it in pressure tanks.

3. Examine the sentence–combining exercises in William Strong's *Sentence Combining: A Composing Book*[9] and Frank

O'Hare's *Sentencecraft: An Elective Course in Writing.*[10] Strong's book is intended for college students and presents essentially unstructured exercises. O'Hare's book is intended for high school students and presents structured exercises. What changes in their exercises would be necessary to adapt them for your students? Prepare some sentence–combining exercises that would be appropriate for your students. How would you explain to your students what they were supposed to do with the exercises?

4. Here is a set of preschoolers' nonstandard spellings from Charles Read's *Children's Categorization of Speech Sounds in English.*[11] What principle did the children apparently apply to organize their spelling system? Why is this research important?

Children's Spelling	Standard Spelling
FEL	feel
LADE	lady
KAM	came
TABIL	table
FAS	face
LIK	like
TIM	time
MISS	mice

5. Using Carol Chomsky's spelling lessons as models, create other similar lessons of the different types.

6. Gather a list of common words of foreign origin whose spelling might cause problems for young students. How can your dictionary help you in compiling your list?

NOTES

[1] *Grammatical Structures Written at Three Grade Levels* (Urbana, Ill.: National Council of Teachers of English, 1965).

[2] *Syntax of Kindergarten and Elementary School Children: A Transformational Analysis* (Urbana, Ill.: National Council of Teachers of English, 1967).

[3] *Transformational Sentence-Combining: A Method for Enhancing the Development of Syntactic Fluency in English Composition* (Urbana, Ill.: National Council of Teachers of English, 1969).

[4] *Sentence Combining: Improving Student Writing without Formal Grammar Instruction* (Urbana, Ill.: National Council of Teachers of English, 1973).

[5] Charles Reed, *Children's Categorization of Speech Sounds in English* (Urbana, Ill.: National Council of Teachers of English, 1975).

[6] "Reading, Writing, and Phonology," *Harvard Educational Review*, 40 (1970), 303.

[7] "Reading, Writing, and Phonology," pp. 304–305.

[8] (Chicago: University of Chicago Press for the Society for Research in Child Development, 1970), pp. 64–67.

[9] (New York: Random House, 1973).

[10] (Lexington, Mass.: Ginn and Co., Xerox Education Group, 1975).

[11] *Children's Categorization of Speech Sounds*, p. 34.

Appendix

Language Arts Textbook Evaluation

The strongest single influence upon teachers is probably the textbook they use. The younger and less experienced the teacher, the greater the power of the textbook. Since teachers often have a voice in textbook selection, they need objective criteria for evaluating the available choices.

In the light of (1) the linguistic information and attitudes presented in the first part of this book, and (2) the linguistically oriented teaching methods presented in the second part of the book, the following evaluation form is suggested for use when selecting language arts textbooks. In order of descending importance, six aspects of language arts textbooks are considered.

The first aspect is the book's attitudes toward language. Superior language arts textbooks build upon the students' native understanding of their language and their previous and current language experiences both inside and outside the classroom. These books include many areas of language study: its history, dialects, dictionaries, and dimensions of usage.

Second, superior textbooks motivate students to learn. The books' ideas interest them and stimulate both inductive and deductive thinking. Such texts describe options for children to choose among; they do not prescribe rules for them to obey.

These books interrelate language study, composition, and literature. They strive for originality, emphasize ideas, and use as little technical linguistic terminology as possible.

Third, superior textbooks are adaptable for various types of students—slow, average, and superior. They can be used with many teaching styles. In other words, they may serve students as reference tools, like dictionaries and atlases; they may supplement the curriculum or they may actually be the prescribed curriculum, guiding instruction.

Fourth, superior textbooks are written in a diction and style suitable to both students and teachers. When tested by a "Cloze Procedure" analysis, they are appropriate for the students for whom they are intended. In addition, they enhance or contrast well with the teacher's own classroom diction and style.

Fifth, superior language arts textbooks reveal clear, effective, and consistent teaching goals, which are explained in the teacher's manual or the introductory comments addressed to the teacher. These goals are reflected in the material actually presented in the text.

Last, and least important, superior texts have excellent miscellaneous features. They contain reference features like a clear table of contents, an adequate index, and appropriate illustrations. In addition, their physical format is practical; the size of the text is appropriate, the paper and binding are sturdy, and the type is easy to read.

Each section of the textbook evaluation form concludes with space for the rater's explanatory notes and comments. At the end of the entire form is a summary sheet, followed by more space for overall explanatory notes and comments.

EVALUATION FORM

Directions for use:
1. In each section indicated by a Roman numeral, place a 3 before each item on which you think the text is outstandingly satisfactory.

2. Place a 2 before each item on which you think the text is more satisfactory than unsatisfactory.

3. Place a 1 before each item on which you think the text is more unsatisfactory than satisfactory.

4. Place a 0 before each item on which you think the text is completely unsatisfactory.

5. Total your points within each section. Record these totals on the Summary Sheet and compare them with those from other textbooks being evaluated. The book having the highest total is the most effective for your purposes.

_____ I. **Attitudes toward Language**

_____ A. How effectively does the text capitalize on students' native understanding of language?

_____ B. How effectively does the text recognize that students may speak various dialects of English?

_____ C. How effectively does the text emphasize that several styles of speech and writing are appropriate to various situations?

_____ D. How effectively does the text emphasize that language changes constantly?

_____ E. How much attention does the text give to teaching reading, writing, listening, and speaking as skills of communication?

_____ F. How much attention does the text give to language as used outside the classroom in television, newspapers, magazines, and advertising?

_____ G. How much attention does the text give to the regional and social dialects of the United States?

_____ H. How much attention does the text give to the history of the English language?

_____ I. How much attention does the text give to the making and using of dictionaries?

_____ J. How clearly does the text explain that dictionaries describe usage and do not prescribe it?

Explanatory Notes and Comments: _____

_____

_____

____ II. **Motivation of Students**

_____ A. How effectively will the text motivate the better students?

_____ B. How effectively will the text motivate the slower students?

_____ C. How effectively will the text encourage inductive thinking?

_____ D. How effectively will the text encourage deductive thinking?

_____ E. How successfully does the text describe options rather than present rules?

_____ F. How well does the text interrelate language study, composition, and literature?

_____ G. How originally does the text present material?

_____ H. How effectively does the text emphasize ideas and minimize linguistic terminology?

Explanatory Notes and Comments: _____

_____

_____

____ III. **Adaptability**

_____ A. How adaptable is the text for slow students?

_____ B. How adaptable is the text for average students?

_____ C. How adaptable is the text for superior students?

_____ D. How adaptable is the text for speakers of non-standard dialects?

_____ E. How useful is the text as a reference tool?

_____ F. How useful is the text as a supplement to the curriculum?

_____ G. How useful is the text as a curriculum guide?

Explanatory Notes and Comments: _____

_____

_____

_____ **IV. Diction and Style**

_____   A. How well will students like the writing style of the text?

_____   B. How accurately is word choice adjusted to the students for whom the text is intended? (Consider using a Cloze test in reaching your conclusions.)

_____   C. How effectively does sentence variety increase the text's appeal?

_____   D. How much will the style of the text enhance your own effectiveness in the classroom?

Explanatory Notes and Comments:_____

_____

_____

_____ **V. Authority and Reliability**

_____   A. How clearly are the instructional goals of the text presented?

_____   B. How effectively do these goals mesh with your own instructional goals?

_____   C. How consistently is the viewpoint of the introductory comments and/or the teacher's manual maintained throughout the text?

Explanatory Notes and Comments:_____

_____

_____

_____ **VI. Miscellaneous Features**

Rate the text on the quality of each of the following.

_____   A.   Reference features
                (table of contents, index, illustrations)
_____   B.   Physical features
                (size, binding, printing, margins, paper)

Explanatory Notes and Comments: _____

_____

_____

_____

SUMMARY SHEET

  I.   Attitudes toward language   _____
 II.   Motivation of students   _____
III.   Adaptability   _____
 IV.   Diction and style   _____
  V.   Authority and reliability   _____
 VI.   Miscellaneous features   _____

Overall Explanatory Notes and Comments: _____

_____

_____

_____

_____

Annotated Bibliography

Bloom, Lois. *Language Development: Form and Function in Emerging Grammars.* Cambridge, Mass.: M.I.T. Press, 1970. Bloom reports her psycholinguistic study of the acquisition of grammar by three children from the ages of 19 to 27 months.

Bloomfield, Leonard and Clarence L. Barnhart. *Let's Read: A Linguistic Approach.* Detroit: Wayne State University Press, 1961. Presents Bloomfield's original system of teaching reading using structural linguistic insights. Contains introductory essays and actual reading lessons.

Bollinger, Dwight. *Aspects of Language.* 2nd ed. New York: Harcourt Brace Jovanovich, 1975. A comprehensive, readable discussion of the nature of language and how it has been and is being studied, with stimulating and creative classroom applications.

Brown, Roger. *A First Language: The Early Stages.* Cambridge, Mass.: Harvard University Press, 1973. Brown, a transformationally oriented psychologist, reports exhaustively on his and his colleagues' research involving three preschool children.

Burling, Robbins. *English in Black and White.* New York: Holt, Rinehart and Winston, 1973. An excellent, short book on regional and social dialects and the educational and social problems implicit in nonstandard black English.

Cazden, Courtney B. *Child Language and Education.* New York: Holt, Rinehart and Winston, 1972. Addressed to all who try to improve children's communication skills through education, the book interweaves methods and findings from linguistics, psycholinguistics, and sociolinguistics to explain both language knowledge and speech performance of children.

Chomsky, Carol. The *Acquisition of Syntax in Children from 5 to 10.* Cambridge, Mass.: M.I.T. Press, 1969. A seminal study of the syntax of forty children in the later stages of language acquisition.

Chomsky, Carol. "Reading, Writing, and Phonology." *Harvard Educational Review,* May 1970, pp. 287–309. This article explores transformational–generative insights into relationships between English sounds and spellings, and relates the theory to the teaching of both spelling and reading.

Cronnell, Bruce. *Beginning Spelling: A Linguistic Review of Six Spelling Series.* Los Alamitos, Calif.: Southwest Regional Laboratory Educational Research and Development, 1971. Compares six commercial spelling series in terms of linguistic orientation, conception of spelling, and treatment of spelling for instruction.

Deighton, Lee C. *A Comparative Study of Spellings in Four Major Collegiate Dictionaries.* Pleasantville, N.Y.: Hardscrabble Press, 1972. Lists variant spellings of more than two thousand words in dictionaries published between 1968 and 1970.

DeStefano, Joanna S., ed. *Language, Society, and Education: A Profile of Black English.* Worthington, Ohio: Charles A. Jones Publishing Co., 1973. This collection of essays on the linguistic, social, and pedagogical implications of black English is keyed to aid teachers in classrooms.

Emery, Donald W. *Variant Spellings in Modern American Dictionaries.* rev. ed. Urbana, Ill.: National Council of Teachers of English, 1973. Lists variant spellings of words in five desk dictionaries published between 1968 and 1973, with an informative introduction explaining categories of variance.

Evans, Bergen. *Comfortable Words.* New York: Random House, 1959. Comments wittily on foibles and fallacies of current English usage, offering guidelines to the use of "easy, simple, comfortable" English.

Foster, Brian. *The Changing English Language.* New York: St. Martin's Press, 1968. An entertaining account of what is happening to the English language, told from the viewpoint of a British lecturer at Southampton University.

Fries, Charles C. *Linguistics and Reading.* New York: Holt, Rinehart and Winston, 1962. Discusses the reading process and the teaching of reading in the light of structural linguistic knowledge. Extends and adapts Bloomfield's system.

Funk, Charles Earle. *A Hog on Ice and Other Curious Expressions.* New York: Harper and Row, 1948. This book and the three following give interesting, amusing stories of the strange histories of common English expressions.

Funk, Charles Earle. *Horsefeathers and Other Curious Words.* New York: Harper and Row, 1958. (See above.)

Funk, Charles Earle. *Thereby Hangs a Tale: Stories of Curious Word Origins.* New York: Harper and Row, 1950. (See above.)

Funk, Wilfred. *Word Origins and Their Romantic Stories.* New York: Grosset and Dunlap, 1950. (See above.)

Gelb, I. J. *A Study of Writing.* Chicago: University of Chicago Press, 1952. A classic, comprehensive presentation of the history of writing from primitive pictures to modern alphabets.

Goodman, Kenneth S., and James T. Fleming, eds. *Psycholinguistics Reading Comprehension Revisited." The Reading Teacher,* October 1973, pp. 6–12. Reversing his widely quoted 1965 hypothesis, Goodman uses miscue analysis to support the position that the only special disadvantage of nonstandard speakers in learning to read is that the teacher rejects their dialects.

Goodman, Kenneth S., ed. *Miscue Analysis: Applications to Reading Instruction.* Urbana, Ill.: Educational Resources Information Center/Clearinghouse on Reading and Communication Skills/National Council of Teachers of English, 1973. Authoritative discussions of miscue research and its applications to the various purposes of a wide variety of teachers and students.

Goodman, Kenneth S., and James T. Fleming, eds. *Psycholinguistics and the Teaching of Reading.* Newark, Del.: International Reading Association, 1969. A collection of papers presented by reading specialists, psychologists, linguists, and psycholinguists on interrelationships among education, psychology, and reading.

Goodman, Yetta M., and Carolyn L. Burke. *Reading Miscue Inventory Manual: Procedure for Diagnosis and Evaluation.* New York: Macmillan, 1972. Most valuable for its explanation of the theory and practice of reading miscue research and its selected annotated bibliography on psycholinguistics and reading.

Hall, Robert A., Jr. *Sound and Spelling in English.* Radnor, Pa.: Chilton Book Co., 1961. A structural linguistic analysis of the spelling system of English as basically alphabetic.

Hanna, Paul R. and others. *Power to Spell, Grades 1–8.* Boston: Houghton Mifflin, 1969. An elementary spelling series incorporating structural linguistic insights.

Hanna, Paul R. and others. *Spelling: Structure and Strategies.* Boston: Houghton Mifflin, 1971. After reviewing theoretical foundations of spelling, the authors explain strategies for developing a modern program leading to "spelling power" for students.

Herndon, Jeanne H. *A Survey of Modern Grammars.* New York: Holt, Rinehart and Winston, 1970 (2nd edition, 1976). Surveys linguistics selectively for language arts teachers, covering traditional, structural, and transformational grammar, dialects, and usage.

Hook, J. N. *The Story of American English.* New York: Harcourt Brace Jovanovich, 1972. Discusses regional dialects in the United States and their historical backgrounds.

Hook, J. N., and Michael G. Crowell. *Modern English Grammar for Teachers.* New York: Ronald Press, 1970. Discusses principles of traditional, structural, and transformational grammar, with emphasis on their relevance to language arts teaching.

Hopper, Robert, and Rita C. Naremore. *Children's Speech: A Practical Introduction to Communication Development.* New York: Harper and Row, 1973. A readable overview of how children learn to talk, explaining how they acquire the sounds, grammar, semantics, and pragmatics of their language.

Huck, Charlotte S. *Children's Literature in the Elementary School.* 3rd ed. New York: Holt, Rinehart and Winston, 1976. A comprehensive, authoritative, well-written, and thoroughly indexed treatment of children's literature. A rich reference-guide for language arts teachers.

Hunt, Kellogg W. *Grammatical Structures Written at Three Grade Levels.* Urbana, Ill.: National Council of Teachers of English, 1965. Reports research on the development of students' grammatical maturity at fourth-, eighth-, and twelfth-grade levels as measured by the "T–unit" (a single independent predication plus its grammatically attached inserts).

Hunt, Kellogg. *Syntactic Maturity in Schoolchildren and Adults.* Chicago: University of Chicago Press for the Society for Research in Child Development, 1970. Extends and verifies Hunt's earlier research on the development of syntactic maturity. Uses controlled writing material that permits direct observation of the exact insertion transformations students use in writing.

Key, Mary Ritchie. *Male/Female Language.* Metuchen, N.J.: Scarecrow Press, 1975. A balanced discussion of both female and male differences in language, written in a highly readable style.

Koch, Kenneth. *Wishes, Lies, and Dreams.* New York: Chelsea House Publishers, 1970. Describes Koch's highly successful experiment in teaching children, grades 1–6, to enjoy writing poetry and to create poems full of imagination and excitement. Includes many examples of children's poems.

Labov, William. *The Social Stratification of English in New York City.* Arlington, Va.: Center for Applied Linguistics, 1966. A classic study of a sociolinguistic approach to the study of dialects.

Labov, William. *The Study of Nonstandard English.* Urbana, Ill.: National Council of Teachers of English, 1970. Labov explains the structured, systematic nature of nonstandard English and suggests ways teachers can observe and teach more accurately in the light of this fact.

Loban, Walter. *Language Development, Kindergarten through Grade 12.* Urbana, Ill.: National Council of Teachers of English, 1976. Final report on Loban's longitudinal study of the language development of 211 children through elementary and secondary school.

Loban, Walter. *The Language of Elementary School Children,* Urbana. Ill.: National Council of Teachers of English, 1963. Loban reports on the first seven years (1952–1959) of his K–12 study of the language development of 338 children by controlled samples of their reading, speaking, and writing. He concludes that students' methods of achieving flexibility within the basic sentence patterns is the clearest measure of their language skill.

Lodwig, Richard, and Eugene F. Barrett. *Words, Words, Words: Vocabularies and Dictionaries.* Rochelle Park, N.J.: Hayden Book Co., 1973. Examines how dictionaries are made and used, and contains many useful teaching suggestions.

Malmstrom, Jean. *Grammar Basics: A Reading/Writing Approach.* 2nd rev. ed. of *An Introduction to Modern English Grammar.* Rochelle Park, N.J.: Hayden Book Co., 1977. Discusses traditional, structural, and transformational grammatical ideas and insights, and relates them to actual use in reading and writing.

Malmstrom, Jean. *Language in Society.* 2nd rev. ed. Rochelle Park, N.J.: Hayden Book Co., 1973. Integrates ideas from linguistic and literary scholarship, psychology, sociology, and anthropology, to illuminate language study for students and teachers.

Malmstrom, Jean, and Barbara Bondar. *Language Alive, Linear A* and *Linear B.* New York: Harper and Row, 1975. These seventh and eighth grade language–composition texts demonstrate how modern linguistic insights can be used dynamically in language arts teaching.

Malmstrom, Jean and Constance Weaver. *Transgrammar: English Structure, Style, and Dialects.* Glenview, Ill.: Scott, Foresman, 1973. An introductory English linguistics text for college students, combining information and insights from traditional, structural, and transformational-generative grammars. The last two chapters, "The Structure of Style" and "The Structure of Dialects," are especially useful as background for language arts teachers.

Mellon, John C. *Transformational Sentence-Combining: A Method for Enhancing the Development of Syntactic Fluency in English Composition.* Urbana, Ill.: National Council of Teachers of English, 1969. Mellon's final report on his pioneer study of seventh graders' accelerated growth toward syntactic fluency uses insights from transformational grammar and practice in sentence-combining.

Menyuk, Paula. *The Acquisition and Development of Language.* Englewood Cliffs, N.J.: Prentice-Hall, 1971. A fairly technical and comprehensive report on psycholinguistic studies of language acquisition. Useful for reference.

Menyuk, Paula. *Sentences Children Use.* Cambridge, Mass.: M.I.T. Press, 1969. Menyuk uses transformational grammar and experimental psychology to describe language acquisition by children from two to seven years of age. She also contrasts normal and abnormal language acquisition.

Moffett, James. *A Student-Centered Language Arts Curriculum, Grades K–13: A Handbook for Teachers.* Boston: Houghton Mifflin, 1968. Moffett views language arts not as a subject but as a unified process by which students expand their ability to communicate.

Myers, L. M. *The Roots of Modern English.* Boston: Little, Brown, 1966. A lucid presentation of the development of the English language. It avoids unnecessary technical details but gives readers a realistic sense of the inevitable tendency of language to change.

O'Donnell, Roy C., William H. Griffin, and Raymond C. Norris. *Syntax of Kindergarten and Elementary School Children: A Transformational Analysis.* Urbana, Ill.: National Council of Teachers of English, 1967. A study of the language of 180 children, K–7, contrasting and describing their growth in controlling sentence structure.

O'Hare, Frank. *Sentence Combining: Improving Student Writing without Formal Grammar Instruction.* Urbana, Ill.: National Council of Teachers of English, 1973. Without learning transformational grammar, O'Hare's seventh-grade students achieved syntactic maturity equal to that of Mellon's seventh graders.

O'Neil, Wayne. "The Spelling and Pronunciation of English." In *The American Heritage Dictionary of the English Language.* William Morris, ed. Boston: American Heritage Publishing Co., Inc. and Houghton Mifflin, 1969, pp. xxxv–xxxvii. A clear, nontechnical explanation of a transformational–generative view of the relationships of English sound to English spelling.

Page, William D., ed. *Help for the Reading Teacher: New Directions in Research.* Urbana, Ill.: Educational Resources Information Center/Clearinghouse on Reading and Communication Skills, National Council of Teachers of English, 1975. Develops implications from recent research on reading behavior. Written in easily understood language, it includes discussions of miscue analysis and Cloze readability tests.

Perron, Jack. "Beginning Writing: It's All in the Mind." *Language Arts,* September 1967, pp. 652–657. This article explains the cognitive rationale of sentence combining and then presents ten interesting and practical classroom–tested, sentence–combining games and activities for young language arts students.

Piaget Jean. *The Language and Thought of the Child.* New York: Harcourt Brace Jovanovich, 1926. This Swiss psychologist describes the stages of the child's cognitive development and holds that the child symbolizes thoughts before translating them into words.

Pooley, Robert C. *The Teaching of English Usage.* Urbana, Ill.: National Council of Teachers of English, 1974. First explaining "the facts about usage" and then "procedures in teaching usage," Pooley continues by giving specific guidelines on usage items important in elementary grades, junior high/middle school, and senior high school levels.

Postman, Neil, and Charles Weingartner. *Linguistics: A Revolution in Teaching.* New York: Dell, 1966. Describes how linguists conduct their inquiries and how these can be translated into classroom activities. A popular book that has had a wide influence.

Quirk, Randolph. *The Use of English.* Enlarged 2nd ed. London: Longmans, Green, 1968. A rich, readable discussion of many aspects of linguistics and modern usage of English throughout the world by the director of the Survey of English Usage in England.

Randolph, Vance, and George P. Wilson. *Down in the Holler: A Gallery of Ozark Folk Speech.* Norman, Okla.: University of Oklahoma Press, 1953. Entertaining and comprehensive discussion of Ozark pronunciation, grammar, and words, and the use of Ozark dialect in fiction.

Roberts, Paul. "A Lot of Latin and Some Greek." In *Understanding English.* New York: Harper and Row, 1958, pp. 356–377. Discusses Greek and Latin roots and affixes, illuminating many facets of English word-building and word-borrowing.

Rosen, Connie, and Harold Rosen. *The Language of Primary School Children.* Baltimore: Penguin Books, 1973. Based on material gathered in England for the School Council Project on Language Development in the Primary School. A lively, practical, humane, and readable explanation of the most promising ways language plays a vital role in children's learning.

Russell, Paula. *An Outline of English Spelling.* Los Alamitos, Calif.: Southwest Regional Laboratory Educational Research and Development, 1975. An exhaustive treatment of phonological and morphological principles of the English spelling system: sound-to-spelling correspondences, lists of common prefixes and suffixes, and rules for combining affixes with base morphemes.

Rutherford, William E. *Sentence Sense.* New York: Harcourt Brace Jovanovich, 1973. This textbook presents a clear, detailed explanation of transformational grammar and is especially useful for its exercises and study questions.

Sapir, Edward. *Language: An Introduction to the Study of Speech.* New York: Harcourt Brace Jovanovich, 1921. A readable classic on the nature of language, especially of English, describing the "drift of the language" toward certain regular patterns of change.

Serjeantson, Mary S. *A History of Foreign Words in English.* London: Routledge and Kegan Paul, 1961. This classic on foreign loanwords in English is a treasury of information for teachers and students.

Shane, Harold G. *Linguistics and the Classroom Teacher.* Washington, D.C.: Association for Supervision and Curriculum Development, 1967. A nonlinguist educator describes the "quiet English revolution" in stringently condensed and sometimes oversimplified terms.

Shores, David L., ed. *Contemporary English: Change and Variation.*

Philadelphia: J. B. Lippincott, 1972. A useful collection of linguistically oriented essays on dialect and usage, with special emphasis on teaching and learning problems.

Shuy, Roger W. *Discovering American Dialects.* Urbana, Ill.: National Council of Teachers of English, 1967. A textbook on dialects in the United States, chiefly regional but with some attention to social variations.

Smith, E. Brooks, Kenneth S. Goodman, and Robert Meredith. *Language and Thinking in School.* 2nd ed. New York: Holt, Rinehart and Winston, 1976. Presents a language-thought-centered view of teaching and learning. The authors interpret and apply insights from recent studies in linguistics and psycholinguistics to the teaching of reading and to other aspects of the curriculum.

Smith, Frank. "Phonology and Orthography: Reading and Writing." *Elementary English,* November 1972, pp. 1075–1088. Examines writing as a language compromise in which neither the writer nor the reader wins. Advantages to the one are disadvantages to the other.

Smith, Frank. *Psycholinguistics and Reading.* New York: Holt, Rinehart and Winston, 1973. A set of important papers on relationships and applications of psycholinguistics to reading and teaching reading, elaborated on and synthesized by the author.

Smith, Frank. *Understanding Reading: A Psycholinguistic Analysis of Reading and Learning to Read.* New York: Holt, Rinehart and Winston, 1971. A technical explanation of psycholinguistic theory on the fundamental aspects of the complex human skill of reading—linguistic, psychological, and physiological.

Strickland, Ruth. *The Language of Elementary School Children: Its Relationship to the Language of Reading Textbooks and the Quality of Reading of Selected Children.* Bulletin of the School of Education, vol. 38, no. 4. Bloomington, Ind.: Indiana University Press, 1962. Using structural linguistic insights, this study investigated the speech of 375 children, grades 1 through 6,, to compare it with the language used in their reading textbooks. Their language was more advanced, showing that texts lag behind children's development of language.

Taylor, Lorenzo D. *Africanisms in the Gullah Dialect.* 1949. Reprint. New York: Arno Press, 1969. The classic linguistic study of the Gullah creole language as it is related to its African roots.

Thorne, Barrie, and Nancy Henley, eds. *Language and Sex: Differences and Dominance.* Rowley, Mass.: Newbury House Publishers, 1975. Varied essays on how language and sex are linked. Includes a comprehensive, well-annotated bibliography.

Trager, George L., and Henry Lee Smith, Jr. *An Outline of English Structure. Studies in Linguistics, Occasional Papers, no. 3.* Norman, Okla.: University of Oklahoma Press, 1951. The classic statement of the Trager–Smith phonemic theory.

Venezky, R. L. "English Orthography: Its Graphical Structure and Its

Relation to Sound." *Reading Research Quarterly*, Winter 1967, pp. 75–106. A linguistically based examination of predictable correspondences between English spelling and the sound system to which it is related.

Vygotsky, L. S. *Thought and Language*. Russian original, 1934. Translated by E. Haufmann and G. Vakar. Cambridge, Mass.: M.I.T. Press, 1962. In the 1930s this Russian psychologist presented important insights into cognitive processes, describing the sequenced stages in word-meaning development.

Wardhaugh, Ronald. *Reading: A Linguistic Perspective*. New York: Harcourt Brace Jovanovich, 1969. Especially useful to language arts teachers for the chapter, "The Spelling System of English," (pp. 97–118), which contains linguistic information that gives insights into the teaching of spelling.

Weir, Ruth. *Language in the Crib*. The Hague: Mouton, 1962. Weir recorded and analyzed the presleep monologues of her two-and-a-half-year-old son, revealing his experimentation with language as he developed it.

Wijk, Axel. *Rules of Pronunciation for the English Language: An Account of the Relationship between English Spelling and Pronunciation*. London: Oxford University Press, 1966. A technical account of the rules that relate English spelling and pronunciation, most interesting to teachers for its chapter on spelling reform proposals.

Index